Praise for Dr. Lisa Longworth and *Cocoon to Butterfly*

"Dr. Longworth takes the reader on an essential life journey from *Cocoon to Butterfly*. Few self-help writers, philosophers, or psychologists have created a clear blueprint for rising from all that binds us in our daily life, to find renewal—a sense of deep purpose. It is the single most important and neglected aspect of our existence and thankfully Dr. Longworth has illuminated the path toward a more fulfilling life. Step by step, with the fluid motion of the butterfly emerging from its cocoon, we can be transformed and the journey is captured perfectly in her book."

Neva Sullaway, *Author of* Chasing Dreamtime

"Lisa Longworth inspires; she revitalizes and regenerates our creativity. Lisa is an artist of the human side of nature who brings out the best in people and helps them experience the joy of life. She has an especially unique gift to work with the gifted. Lisa is a healer's healer."

Jonas Salk, M.D., *Founder of the Salk Institute*
Discoverer of the Salk vaccine against Polio

"Cocoon to Butterfly—is an inspiring book to read and a powerful process for creating your own breakthroughs to reinvent your life or your purpose. Through her own transformational life experience, Lisa weaves a method each of us can use to break out of our own cocoon and reach higher points in our lives. The book is sprinkled with illustrations to help readers find their own path toward positive change and greater fulfillment. I heartily gift this book to my friends, clients, and others who want to elevate the quality of their lives."

Dr. Peter T. Lambrou, *Author of* Code to Joy, Instant Emotional Healing, *and* Self-Hypnosis: The Complete Manual for Health and Self Change

"As a psychologist for over 40 years, the majority of my clients describe feeling stuck and unfulfilled in their lives whether it is their lifestyle, career, or relationships. Cocoon to Butterfly elegantly articulates the metamorphosis process of a butterfly as a model to inspire and guide people in transforming their lives. I highly recommend this powerful book to my clients going through midlife change."

Dr. Michael R. Samko, Licensed psychologist and hypnosis expert, personally trained by the renowned Dr. Milton Erickson

"*Cocoon to Butterfly, Creative Midlife Change for the Busy Person*, is truly a tour de force, a montage of eastern philosophy, art, nature, poetry and modern therapy. Dr. Longworth merges these seamlessly into an enjoyable narrative that encourages the reader to find his or her path toward living a more mindful existence."

Dr. Lawrence A. Herzog, Professor of Urban Design, School of Public Affairs, San Diego State University, California

"This is a deeply profound yet accessible book. *Cocoon to Butterfly* helps the reader move through their process of personal transformation with grace, ease and a sense of playfulness and joy!"

Dr. Marion Moss Hubbard, author of **Work as a Heroic Journey** *and the* **Heroic Path to Self-Forgiveness**

"*Cocoon to Butterfly*—what a gift of beauty, generosity, and guiding Light! This book has the juicy quality of being both sublimely accessible yet potent. I especially appreciate Longworth's emphasis on "creative tension," encouraging us to be with the discomfort of the change process; and her support to shape the practices as our own. Count me in for using this process to check-in with my Psyche and Soul!"

Meo O'Malley, Creator of **Altars Within: sacred space in daily life**, *artist, teacher curriculum leader with k-12 Arts education*

"This book is a revelation! It helps people make their unconscious conscious and thus allows control of one's behavior. She shows us how to make all work be play. As I read her book, I began flapping my 90-year old slightly worn-at-the-edges butterfly wings. Lisa's book made me happy."

Dr. Natasha Josefowitz, Author of 20 books including her most recent, Living Without the One You Cannot Live Without: Hope and Healing after Loss

"Savor this book like fine wine. The author is so present with her message that sometimes it feels like she is helping turn pages. A delightful read."

Richard A. Hubbard, Former President, National Association of Consumer Protection Investigators

"Lisa Longworth is a consultant who lives her life as an art form; and as a human being embodies rare congruency. I highly recommend her work."

Paul Brenner, M.D., Ph.D., Lecturer, Author, **Health is a Question of Balance**

"Lisa is a master of the art of the possible. She uses her enthusiasm, warmth, focus and intelligence to lift our head out of the sand of everyday obligations and help us envision creative ways of living and working. She is a gifted woman."

Dr. Warren Farrell, Bestselling Author, **The Myth of Male Power & Why Men are The Way They Are**

Cocoon to Butterfly®

Creative Midlife Change
for the Busy Person

Nancy,
Honoring your
gifts of
connection.
may you continue
to Love Life
even more!

Cocoon
to
Butterfly®

Creative Midlife Change
for the Busy Person

Dr. LISA LONGWORTH

TWIN WING

Copyright © 2019 by Dr. Lisa Longworth

All Rights Reserved. No part of this publication may be reproduced, stored in or introduced into a retrieval system, or transmitted in any form or by any means (electronic, mechanical, photocopied, recorded of otherwise), without the prior written permission of both the copyright owner and the publisher of this book, except by a reviewer who wishes to quote brief passages in connection with a review written for insertion in a magazine, newspaper, broadcast, website, blog or other outlet.

COCOON TO BUTTERFLY is a Registered Trademark.
Reg. No. 5,674,154, First use 6-1-1986

Second Edition

ISBN-10: 0-9985081-7-9
ISBN-13: 978-0-9985081-7-7

Library of Congress Control Number: 2016921483

Cocoon to Butterfly is published by:

TWIN WING

For information please direct emails to:
info@twinwing.com

Cover art by Dr. Lisa Longworth. "Golden Flight," painting on silk with acrylic, silk dyes, mixed media, 2' x 6'.
All artwork in this book has been created by the author (paintings, sculptures, mixed media, drawings) with the exception of the photo on page 9. Visit www.LisaLongworth.com to learn more about her art.

Cover design: Teri Rider
Book layout and typography: Teri Rider and Associates
Desktop Publisher 2nd Ed.: Zach McDermott

Printed in the United States of America

Dedication

**"Let intuition be your guide,
with reason by its side."**

~Jonas Salk, M.D.

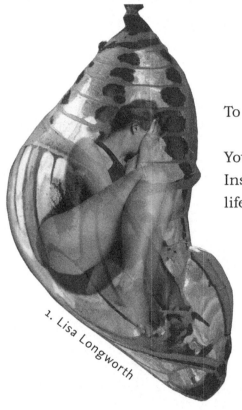

1. Lisa Longworth

To Jonas, my spiritual father,

You encouraged me to trust myself,
Inspiring my Cocoon to Butterfly
life's work to take flight.

To the Beloved Reader,
This book is dedicated to your unfolding wings,
May you soar into the life of your dreams.

the *Cocoon to Butterfly®* process

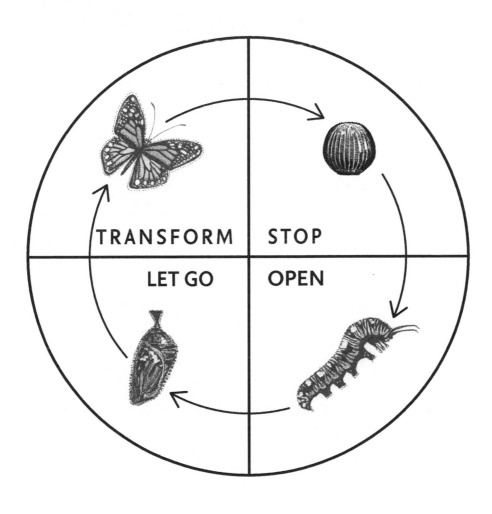

TRANSFORM   STOP

LET GO   OPEN

INTRODUCTION

egg

23

2   **BE PRESENT** FOCUS YOUR LENS OF
PERCEPTION 45

caterpillar

73

COCOON
103

butterfly
123

CONCLUSION 157

"The butterfly signals change,
transformation, balance,
grace, beauty and spirituality.
In Christianity the butterfly
was a symbol of the soul.
In China it was a symbol of
conjugal bliss and joy.
The butterfly asks us not to
take life too seriously.
Remember to dance as it brings
back the sweetness of life.
Change can occur but it does not have
to be so traumatic,
it can occur gently,
naturally, and joyfully."

~Tim O'Reilly

2. Lisa Longworth

Cocoon or Chrysalis?

Chrysalis is the scientific name for the container that the butterfly emerges from and the cocoon is the name of the container from which a moth emerges.

Cocoon to Butterfly is my creative name for the metamorphosis process of the soul's journey—one that follows an organic path connected deeply to our inner nature and the natural world.

3. Lisa Longworth

Introduction

The *Cocoon to Butterfly* process

The *Cocoon to Butterfly* process is focused on creating the life you really want, one that is handcrafted, soul-centered, authentically your own, created from the inside out. This book will help you access your creative resources to make life changes so you can listen more deeply to yourself and life. You will become aware of your old skin, or *Cocoon*, that you need to *Let Go* of to emerge as the *Butterfly* of your own *Becoming*.

The process is about honoring cycles and seasons of life. It is based on an earth-centered life cycle paradigm.

Some people have believed that the world was made for humans, and humans were made to rule it. Now is the time to see yourself more as a strand in the web of life on earth rather than the ruler of the web. Your silky strand of luminosity in this living web is meant to shine. Our world depends on it. Spread your gossamer wings and fly!

Note to Readers about Capitalization:

When referring to the metaphor of the *Cocoon* or the *Butterfly*, (as in the *Cocoon to Butterfly* work), it is capitalized and italicised in this book. It is not capitalized nor italicised when referring to the insect itself.

1. ***STOP*** Face the Unknown. Renew Vital Energy

2. ***BE PRESENT*** Focus your Lens of Perception, Renew with Meditation & Silence

3. ***OPEN*** Align with inner seeing & inner hearing, Listen to Images & Intuition

4. ***ALLOW*** Embrace discomfort, Nourish Allowing Creative Tension

5. ***LET GO*** Release everything that you are not, Surrendering to Your Larger Life

6. ***SIMPLIFY*** Transform by doing less, Simplify, Simplify, Simplify

7. ***TRANSFORM*** Freedom & joy in higher awareness, Play, Gratitude & Generosity

---

The beginning

My heart was exploding. At 19 years old, minutes away from undergoing life-threatening brain surgery, I was sitting in my hospital bed. My doctors had told me most likely I would either die from the surgery or be a quadriplegic, but that wasn't affecting me at that moment. My heart had been blasted open by love. One by one, my boyfriend, my family, and my closest friends had come into my hospital room to say goodbye.

That moment set me free. My fear of death had been blown away by the power of love. I knew if I died from the surgery, my life would be complete and whole. Fourteen hours later when I woke up, I had survived four brain surgeons cutting out a tumor from my lower cerebellum during a five-hour surgery, with no complications, making medical history at the time in the late seventies. I was thrilled that I would not live the rest of my life in a wheelchair, as I was physically whole. However, something had happened to me that would change me forever. I had a near-death-experience.

This book is directly connected to what I encountered during my near-death-experience. At 19 years old, I broke free of a *Cocoon*. Since then, I have spent my lifetime helping people fully express their deepest self through my *Cocoon to Butterfly* process, a process especially helpful at midlife.

Creative midlife change or reinvention in midlife, (between 35 and 65 years old), has predictable patterns. These patterns are mirrored in all of *Nature*. It is natural when you are in the middle of a big change to feel lost. Yet, if you can take your time to slow down and align yourself with *Nature*, both your own nature and the *Nature* of life, you will be carried on your journey by a larger life force. Doors will open where there were no doors before. Like an emerging butterfly stuck in the cocoon, flowing with the process rather than struggling against it *allows* it to unfold naturally.

For me, death was a teacher that put me more in touch with life. In the almost four decades since then, I have watched myself and my clients continually change. Shedding the old *Cocoon* skin of their past, they learn how to creatively navigate their journey and emerge into a more fully alive life.

Change is hard, especially the older we get. We are used to doing things a certain way and it can be difficult to reinvent new patterns. We lack clear maps that show us how to get there, wherever "there" is. It is difficult sometimes to make major life changes when you can't see where you are going—when there are no signposts on the road. If you are in midlife, important changes occur that are invisible.

June Cutright, a 46-year-old corporate executive at Microsoft for twelve years, suddenly felt lost and empty. In our first session, she asks, "Is this all there is?" While discussing her current life situation, June suddenly realizes all the invisible changes that have occurred. Her twelve years of climbing the corporate ladder have paid off—she is at the top of her game, both professionally and financially. June's *Cocoon to Butterfly* drawings reveal a deep rut she hadn't realized she was in, and the way out is for her to access a lightness of being (*Butterfly* drawing of a radiant sun—see below). This information becomes an image-based map revealing her path to reinvent her life.

For June, her creative midlife change that started in a "rut" (see her drawing and story above) and ended with a kind of "radiance" was a complete surprise for her. She, by her own admission, would have never thought her spiritual side would open so spontaneously. By following the program, especially the three steps of *Be Present, Open* and *Let Go*, an inner light she calls the "Luminous One" was revealed inside of her. The best tool for her was the *C2B (Cocoon to Butterfly) Journal* where she would write after meditating every morning. She got in touch with an inner guidance that spoke clearly to her. The idea of living a simpler life came up again and again. As a result, she made a step down on the ladder at Microsoft to a less stressful position that *allows* her more time to *Listen* to the "Luminous One" and create a more spacious radiant life for herself. In our last session, she laughed out loud and said, "I now know much more of myself than when we started. And there is so much more to discover. I have the tools to dig deeper and fly higher."

Like June, in midlife, we shift from one game to another without being given the rules. It can be likened to how the caterpillar must feel when its world radically shifts and it dissolves into a cocoon.

Your change tools

Getting unstuck is challenging if you don't have the tools to find your path. The change tools in this book support the natural creative process of your own unfolding. In my own life, I continue to reinvent myself. I have evolved as an artist, counselor, teacher, and writer, letting go of my former old skin to become fully alive and connected to what matter most in my life. This book shares my soul's journey to express my deepest passion and to help others to do the same.

The creative process heals us and reveals our true nature. I am grateful to have been a pioneer in the field of Creative Process since the mid-1980s. At the University of California San Diego Extension, I helped develop the Art and the Creative Process department, bringing students never-before-offered creativity classes. In my years as the head of the Expressive Art Therapy department at International University of Professional Studies, my masters and doctorate students, again and again, used their intuition and creativity, not only for their education but also as a way of life. They used the creative process as a spiritual, psychological, and creative path to personally change and serve life. The change tools in this book have naturally evolved from what has worked with thousands of my students and clients over decades of working together.

Are you ready for change, if only you had the time to figure it out?

If you are a busy person ready to reinvent your life, you've come to the right place. The challenge is you must start by *stopping*. This is hard for most busy people! These simple change tools help you *Stop, Open, Let Go and Transform* your life.

The process of change can be confusing and miserable, or it can be a daring time to trust your heart and passionately follow your own creative process. If you feel trapped, it can seem difficult to become unstuck.

What if you could instantly shift from confusion to clarity by accessing a different part of your brain? Often we automatically use the rational, thought-based part of our brains when we're mapping out our life changes instead of accessing our intuitive, creative, image-based parts of our brain. This book will guide you to access a larger part of yourself to both envision your change and learn how to navigate it.

Perhaps your life change is simply an organic, natural process, like the breaking open of the *Cocoon* to become the *Butterfly.* An important part of the process is recognizing the patterns you may have lived all your life, but are keeping you stuck in your *Cocoon*—then choosing to let them go, like old skin, to create the life you want.

"Midway upon the journey of our life, I found myself within a forest dark, for the straightforward pathway had been lost."

~Dante Alighieri, *The Divine Comedy*

Dante's "forest dark" is like the stuck *Cocoon* my clients find themselves in when they first come into my office. As natural a cycle as puberty, we go through a massive reinvention of ourselves "midway upon the journey of our life."

Your creative life will probably continue to reinvent itself many times over the decades of your adulthood. I love Dante's quote about being lost and stuck because it is a natural process in living a great life.

"Nature thinks everywhere alike."
~Ancient Vedic Saying

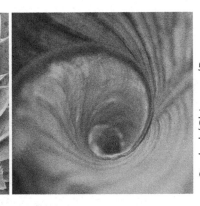

4. Stedrak/Chinnery/Ross

The metamorphosis of the butterfly is a map for your journey

Align with *Nature* and you align with your own true nature. *Nature's* most magical changing creature, the butterfly, offers us an organic navigational chart for our own creative midlife change. Our Western world, religions and much of our American culture have become separated from nature. We tend to lead our lives with our head and less by trusting our body, the ground of our individual self.

"Learning about the natural world is one thing. Learning from the natural world that is the switch. That is the profound switch."

~Janine Benyus

Beginning as an egg on a leaf, the butterfly teaches us to *Stop* ourselves and *Be Present* in a safe container. Then we learn the importance of both *Allowing* and *Opening* more deeply as the emerging creature becomes a caterpillar eating its way along. As the *Cocoon*, we learn the power of *Letting Go*. The caterpillar has *Let Go* of its body that has become a liquid soup for the butterfly's imaginal cells to eat. Finally, as the wet wings of the butterfly emerge and take flight, the last change principle arises-*Transform*.

"The goal of life is to make your heartbeat match the beat of the universe, to match your nature with Nature."

~Joseph Campbell

The 4-phases of change in the butterfly's life: the egg, caterpillar, cocoon and butterfly, mirror the 4-stages of creative midlife change. I truly believe *Nature* does unfold everywhere alike! Your change process can be difficult or you can flow with life's changes the way *Nature* does.

The egg, the first phase of the butterfly's life, mirrors our ability to contain or hold the changes ahead of us. To be like the butterfly's egg, we focus on holding space and boundaries for our journey of change.

In Step One, we explore the power of *Stop*, the first essential tool in changing ourselves. The secret ingredient in the change tool *Stop* is that it helps us interrupt our patterns of life, gaining access to a larger resource of energy than we have in our normal day-to-day lives.

We must choose to *Stop*, wherever we are, whatever we are doing and simply be *Present*. We diminish our access to the full spectrum of life force available to us when we are not present in life. Yet we live in a busy, action-oriented culture where most people find it difficult to *Stop*.

Thinking with the rational mind is important; however, we must shift our inner leadership from our head to our gut and our heart. The first step is to *Stop* ourselves so we have the additional life force to make the changes we need to make.

Step Two explores the power to *Be Present*. This change tool empowers our ability to refocus and relax into silence and experience the quality of truth by being still. We discover our natural facility to release our noisy inner mind chatter and connect to the peaceful place within ourselves. When we are *Present* we have the power to access much more of our natural intelligence and wisdom.

In the Caterpillar phase, the focus is on our ability to consume food for our soul. A caterpillar is an eating machine. The soul food you eat is enhanced through new ways of *Opening* to your essential self, as well as your ability to *Allow* the movement of your journey to carry you. As you *Allow* the creative tension to be uncomfortable, the movement of your journey is accelerated.

In Step Three, we explore new ways to *Open*—not to our automatic endless mind chatter, but to our intuition—feelings we have in our gut and the images that arise in our mind's eye. We must listen to be centered with our very essence, our soul. In listening to our deepest self, we experience the quality of connection that loosens all stuck places.

Step Four is an invitation into the power and principle of *Allowing*. To live our free and authentic life, the *Butterfly* of our own *Becoming*, we must *Allow* it to be as it is. *Allowing* becomes a change tool when you can accept whatever arises in the moment. By directly facing tension and emotional pain without covering it up to be safe and comfortable, you naturally open up a tremendous wellspring of creativity.

In the *Cocoon* phase, we explore the idea of *Letting Go*. In the cocoon, the old form of the caterpillar literally dissolves into a liquid soup that feeds the journey of the metamorphosis of the changing insect. To evolve into the *Butterfly* of our own *Becoming* we must surrender or *Let Go*, which is the focus of Step Five. When we *Let Go* we experience the spiritual quality of surrender.

In the emerging *Butterfly* phase, we focus on celebration. The final two steps mirror our own creative process of unfolding our own wings. To fly, we must take ourselves lightly using the *Simplify* change tool in Step Six. You will discover how to do less and let life be easy. We experience the gift of peace by *simplifying* our lives.

In Step Seven, we explore the power of *Transformation* that naturally occurs when we are connected to our essential self. In the spirit of fun and *Play*, life is flowing through us with a kind of effortless ease. I call it *Play* because pure joy is present. It is not avoidance or "playing hooky" from what we are supposed to be doing. This kind of *Play* is about being in the flow of life, living full out, with passion and purpose. The attitude of gratitude is *Present*. Through *Play*, we experience the quality of beauty in the joy that is *Present* as life dances through us.

The 21st century is a time of unprecedented radical change with the constant dissolving of old forms and the unfolding of new ones. Our ability to be successful and flow with these changing times is greatly enhanced by using these change tools in the *Cocoon to Butterfly* method. They empower us to harmonize with our essential self as we reinvent our daily life.

If you feel you are here for a reason and are attempting to emerge into your next season, then this book is for you. Ready to begin?

How to use this book

In my many years of leading groups and individuals towards the *Butterfly* of their own *Becoming*, I have found that those who use daily and weekly Change Tools make breakthroughs.

- Read one chapter a week

- Write and draw in your *C2B (Cocoon to Butterfly) Journal* every day

- Use your *Butterfly* images and words regularly (from your *Cocoon to Butterfly* drawing and writing)

- Develop your own Signature Practice, keeping it fresh through experimentation to discover what works best for you now and in the future

- Write your responses to the Check-In questions at the end of each week in your *C2B Journal*

The two most important tools

Using the tools in this book accelerates your *transformation*. The two most important tools are working with your personal *Cocoon to Butterfly* symbols that will come out of the drawing process and daily writing in your *C2B Journal*. Using all of the tools will give you deeper self-understanding and clarity.

"We delight in the beauty of the butterly, but rarely admit the changes it has gone through to achieve that beauty."

~Maya Angelou

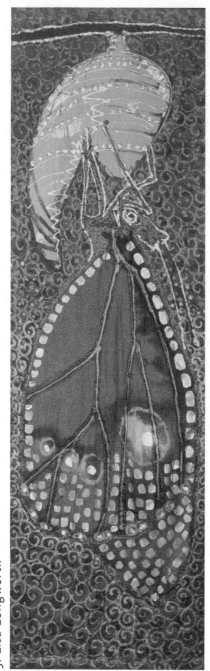

5. Lisa Longworth

Here are the tools and exercises you will work with:

- *C2B (Cocoon to Butterfly) Journal*
- *Cocoon to Butterfly* Sacred Place
- Retreats
- *Entering Presence Meditation*
- *Butterfly Breathing*
- *Freedom Meditation*
- *Cocoon to Butterfly* drawings
- Words and stories from your drawings
- Non-dominant Hand Writing
- Genius Council
- Mentors
- Witnessing Consciousness
- Recognizing Barriers that Keep you Stuck
- *Simplifying* Life
- From Multitasking to *Simplicity*
- Youngster Yoga (to Play)
- Laughter Yoga (to Play)
- Islands of Time to Play
- Gratitude through Writing
- Gratitude through Speaking
- Gratitude in Random Moments
- Gratitude through Art and Movement
- *Nature* Time
- Cultivating Solitude

Signature Practice

Your Signature Practice

In this book, you will learn how to cultivate the best change tools to deepen your metamorphosis process. Your Signature Practice is your custom-designed inner workout to develop the muscles of your creativity and connection to your soul. You will evolve your practice until it becomes your own Signature Practice. Over a lifetime, certain practices, such as journaling, may fall away and other ones, such as meditation, may become primary.

Cupcakes or creative change?

*Are you willing to develop your
Intention, Commitment, and Discipline?
Even if the taste isn't always so sweet?*

Many people love self-help books. They eat them up like cupcakes at a birthday party in the roaring cacophony that sounds like they are changing but in reality is only noise. Self-help reading can become a form of entertainment, like party favors, rather than a tool for personal *transformation*. Living unconsciously, according to old habits, can lead to a mid-life crisis or a miserable life.

Do you recognize yourself as a "cupcake eater," and are you willing to approach this book, and your daily life, differently? If so, you will opt for creative change knowing that the *Cocoon to Butterfly* process requires intention, commitment, and discipline. Creativity is like a muscle that can be developed and needs exercise. This book will help you develop your ability to creatively change.

Did you know?

Butterfly eggs are usually laid in a protective environment near plants that the soon-to-be caterpillar will eat. These eggs come in many colors and shapes, including oval, spherical or pod shaped; with colors most commonly of yellow, white and green.

the *Cocoon to Butterfly* process
Egg = STOP

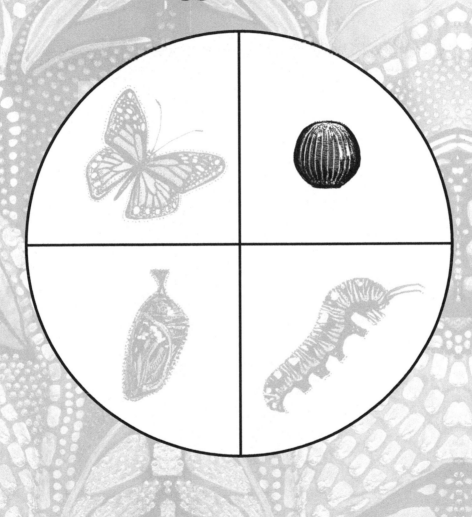

egg

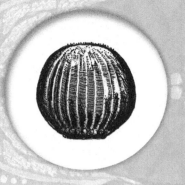

Create New Boundaries and Still the Mind

The Egg begins the first of four incarnations in the butterfly's metamorphosis as it swaps one body for an almost entirely new one.

1 STOP

The transformative shell or container of the butterfly's egg breathes. Our first meal, in our *Cocoon to Butterfly* personal change journey, is *Stopping* to *Renew* vital energy.

2 BE PRESENT

This mirrors the human being's metamorphosis in the creative midlife journey, when making authentic change requires *Stopping* automatic behaviors, such as our mind chatter.

1 STOP

FACE THE UNKNOWN
RENEW VITAL ENERGY

"If you watch how *Nature* deals with adversity, continually *renewing* itself, you can't help but learn."

~Bernie Siegel

"*Nature* has the power to *renew* and refresh."

~Helen Keller

Renewal is essential to life. Nature *stops* and restores itself—why is it so difficult for us to do it? Many of us have lost our natural internal gauge to know when our vital energy tanks are running on empty. We don't know when to *stop* and retreat or do whatever it takes to refill ourselves. Our consumer entertainment-oriented culture offers lots of opportunities to fill up on movies, TV, video games, and shopping. Our digital age offers a sense of instant connection to our friends and family. However, sometimes refueling with these kinds of contemporary choices still leaves us feeling lost and empty.

One of the biggest challenges in my private practice is supporting busy professionals in slowing down and deeply listening to themselves. It doesn't have to take a lot of time to slow down, it can happen in three minutes or less. Busy professionals often have early patterning that equates performance and achievement to establishing a safe connection with life. To put it another way, to secure a safe attachment, a child learns to be "good" and to do what the parent wants. Many of us have these intense inner patterns that we must become conscious of if we are to grow our wings and soar.

The metaphor of the butterfly is a powerful one, especially as you are going through change. Its metamorphosis mirrors the alchemy of our own life changes, as the creature changes bodies four times, from egg to caterpillar, to cocoon and finally to butterfly.

Building a container for your changing self

This first section of the book represents the initial phase of a butterfly's life cycle. The butterfly starts out its life as an egg, and once it is laid, it eats its shell for its first meal. As we reinvent ourselves, we begin a new life as well; we need a container for our changing self. We *Stop* and rest in a place to *Renew*, and like the butterfly's egg, the first meal of our journey refuels our vital energy.

Making time for your solitude

In this first phase of the metamorphosis process, you will learn how to make time for solitude, *Nature*, and meditation—time that will help you develop your personal signature practice.

Signature symbols and stories to guide you

Each person has his or her own signature symbols and stories that authentically guide them on their path. One way to access these symbols and stories is through the *Cocoon to Butterfly* process.

The process helps clarify one's current situation, especially focusing on the challenges or feelings of being stuck or frustrated, the *Cocoon*; and then what it might look like to move into the next level of life, the *Butterfly* of one's own *Becoming*.

Once both the current challenging circumstances and future desired outcome are clarified through either dialogue with the counselor or in writing with oneself, then a quick scribble drawing is made to depict the *Cocoon's* energy, followed by a second drawing of the *Butterfly's* energy. Each drawing is spontaneously named and then a story is told from both drawings. All of this information is recorded and used in the months to come as entrance points to access inner knowing.

Getting clear about your challenges

In the *Cocoon to Butterfly* process, we begin our first session by getting clear about the challenges of our circumstances. This includes frustrations and feelings of being stuck and unable to move forward. These frustrations and challenges are expressed in the *Cocoon* drawing, which is done first. Drawing can be a powerful vehicle to express frustrations and feelings as illustrated in the following story.

When my 54-year-old client, Jill Hansen, came in for her first session, she talked about feeling slightly depressed, that the best years of her life might be behind her. A petite redhead with sparkling eyes, Jill was soft spoken and smiled a lot. Her midsection was round, but her arms were slender and active as she talked about her frustrations. "Since menopause, I have become complacent and tired. My biggest passion is reading romance novels on my Kindle in the living room. My husband Joe makes fun of me and says I am a couch potato. Frankly, I don't care what he thinks. I am living my life the way I want to." With those last words, her voice trembled and she started to sob.

"I am not living my life, Dr. Longworth, I am just existing and I know I escape through my romance novels and feeding my face with food. But I am stuck."

She went on to tell me that both she and her husband, Joe, were security focused, choosing stability over excitement in their work and lives. Now at 54, her job felt like a dead end, but she was afraid to try anything else. I asked her to draw a *Cocoon* drawing of her stuck place. It looked like a small dark box at the bottom of the paper. She titled it "Prison."

The *Butterfly Self* drawing was very different. At first, when she started to draw, picking up a red marker, she *stopped*. "I can't do this. I have no idea what it looks like to emerge from my stuck place." Then I encouraged her to *Stop* talking and trust the creative process of the scribble drawing. It took several rounds of her interrupting her drawing process to talk and explain her inability to complete the process before her simple drawing emerged.

The *Butterfly Self* drawing had a small yellow flame in the center. There was green on the bottom and a light blue sky on top. She named it, "The Fire is Alive and Burning."

Then I asked her to tell me a story about both of her drawings. She said the "Prison" is a dark, damp, miserable place that she lives in. "See, the little box has no doors or windows. It is a prison with no escape. I don't know why that is so, but it is. Well, that's funny that I used the word 'escape,' because I know I do escape for hours every day through my romance novels."

In telling a story about the other side of her paper, her *Butterfly Self*, Jill said, "This little flame is small and very powerful. It lights up the world when it burns." Pointing up to the blue sky in her drawing she continued, "the vast sky above holds the little flame as does the green earth below. There is both peace and passion in this place." She whispered to me, "my inner fire is alive and burning. I just can't feel it."

I asked Jill, "When your fire is alive and burning, what is that like?" She paused for the longest time, her pensive eyes darting back and forth pondering the question. "I am sad to say, I am not sure what it is like to be in touch with my inner fire."

The next step she took was to create time every day just for her creative mid-life change, not work or tending to Joe or reading romance novels. She focused on her

Cocoon to Butterfly process in her words from "Prison" to "the fire is alive and burning." She set up an outer space that *transformed* the table next to her couch, where she normally had her cup of tea while reading. On it, she put her *Journal*, wrapped in a blue scarf; she said to keep it more private and sacred. She bought a special candle and a large rough metal key she found in an antique store. "The key is my way out of prison, and the candle, of course, represents my fire! Although I don't feel it burning inside me yet, it is a symbolic gesture I love."

In our sessions, we talked about how Jill might *Renew* herself. She was exploring taking a health retreat where she could focus on diet and exercise. She struggled with spending the money for such a retreat, but she finally found one locally which would support her goals. Boldly, she took a week off from work and went on retreat at Golden Health Spa, where she took classes, exercised, and was counseled in how to have a healthy lifestyle. Later she described her experience as the best week of her life, which completely made her future metamorphosis possible.

Constructing your supportive plan

When she returned from her retreat, she was on fire! We worked together to construct a supportive plan to keep that fire burning in her life. "I used to have a lot of judgment about those fitness type people who are always running to the gym. But the daily support on the retreat opened up something in me and now I do have more energy than before. I don't want to go back to spending so much time on my couch anymore."

Jill's favorite workouts were long walks with friends in the neighborhood. She was building strong friendships, which had been missing, in her life. She and Joe had been together for over 30 years and she often felt bored around him. "I hate to say this, Dr. Longworth, but I think Joe is part of my prison and the marriage contributes to my depression."

Jill's doctor felt she was not clinically depressed, but he was willing to prescribe anti-depressants. "I want to work on our program and not take drugs to rekindle my fire," Jill said. Her body was strengthened through exercise and diet, plus she had more friends now. But her self-expression was absent from her program. "I am working on my *Journal*, but I must admit to being a little bored with writing about myself." Tuning into Jill, I asked, "What about writing fiction, Jill? Why don't you give that a try?"

Well, the rest is history. Jill Hansen is now publishing her third romance novel. She is so on fire with writing; their old guest room is now her writing room. She is planning on giving notice at work once her advance comes through from her publisher.

6. Lisa Longworth

Creating your own place for *transformation*

In graduate school, I studied trance and dance and mask making for several months in Bali, Indonesia. The Balinese have the concept Desa, Kala, and Patra. Desa means place, Kala is time, and Patra is subject or circumstance. This reflects the importance of place, time, and circumstance in living life and how changing any one of those things can change the whole.

Mirrored in the life of the butterfly, the place an egg is laid can influence the life of that butterfly. The place is important. I just returned from a trip to Burma, in Southeast Asia, spending time in hundreds of ancient temples and feeling the power of these places for people to connect to what matters most to them. The place is important.

Creating a special place in your home for your developing self is a powerful act that supports your *transformation*. Like the Balinese concept of Desa, finding a place to put a few meaningful objects to honor the sacred unfolding of your life is powerful.

Exercise: *Cocoon to Butterfly* sacred place

Create a special space in your home for your changes. As you start to make big changes on the inside of yourself, it can be powerful to create a small and special place in your home to honor those changes. It can be a table in your bedroom or another room where you clear away the ordinary things that are currently on it and find a few items that mirror the *transformational* journey you are currently on. You can keep this book on that space as a start.

In my work with Jill, I asked her where in her home she could imagine putting her "*Cocoon to Butterfly* Place" for our work together. She closed her eyes and giggled. She had immediately pictured in her imagination her maternal grandmother Sadie's oak table. Then she told me how Sadie was an oil painter and how close she felt to her, even after her death ten years ago. In the next session, Jill told me she had cleared away this table in her den and put her *Cocoon to Butterfly* drawing and some bright colored felt pens on the table alongside her new journal.

"I look at it every day, and it makes me feel good," Jill exclaimed in our next session. I told her how important it could be to have an outer place in our home to hold the inner space of our journey. We go to churches for religious experiences, shopping centers for buying experiences, college campuses for educational experiences—so creating a small space for your *transformational* experience is powerful.

Ideas:

- Find a table somewhere in your home—in your bedroom or another room. A semi-private place where you can put items over the weeks of your journey that are significant to you. Participants in my groups have called these items "Soul Medicine" and their space an "Artist Altar."

- Keep the space fresh by cleaning it, intuitively rearranging the items regularly and adding new things to it.

- Find creative ways to "feed" your place. Consider adding some small living thing to it on a daily basis, such as a leaf or fresh flower.

- Consider finding or letting objects "find" you that are metaphors for your journey, such as a candleholder or totem animal statue, and adding that to your place.

- If inspired to create visual art, add felt pens, colored pencils or paints as a symbol of your creativity flourishing.

- Some of my clients find a theme song for their *transformational* journey, so a copy of that song on your music player or that song's lyrics can be kept in that space. Other clients have special words, often the name of the *Butterfly Self*, that they write on paper and place in their special space.

7. Lisa Longworth

EXERCISE: C2B (Cocoon to Butterfly) Journal

The perfect companion to this book is the Cocoon to Butterfly Journal, a 7-week Proven Course to breakthrough life challenges. (For more information go to page 167) Used it in conjunction with this book, the C2B Journal supports strengthening your inner voice and authentic self. You may also use any kind of journal that you wish for your C2B Journal. The key is to start and consistently work every day.

"Opportunities to find deeper powers within ourselves come when life seems most challenging."

~Joseph Campbell

A painting retreat in the mountains served as a powerful part of my soul's journey. At 24-years-old, I was a year away from finishing my bachelor's degree at University of California San Diego. For a week, I studied painting with artist Francoise Gilot. A powerful artist in her own right, deeply spiritual, and highly intelligent, she may be best known as Paloma Picasso's mother, as she bore two of Pablo Picasso's children in their 10-year relationship. I admired her independent brilliance.

8. Lisa Longworth

Somehow in the power of her presence, I felt safe to share my near-death experience, one that I had *Cocooned* within me and had not shared with anyone for over four years. Months after my experience, verbally sharing my vision with others had disconnected me and made people concerned that I had lost my marbles and needed to see a psychiatrist. So to keep safe and connected to my family and friends, I *stopped* trying to share the experience and instead chose to survive. I decided to focus on being a good student and getting straight A's, but deep inside of me there was a huge hole. I felt like I was missing something.

I was *renewed* by *stopping* my regular life as a student and venturing into a painting retreat in the local Idyllwild mountains. Finally, I gained the confidence to share my near-death experience with Francoise and she seemed to completely get it. I knew she understood. I could feel it in my bones. Then, without hesitation, she said, "OK, now go paint."

So in the safety of her art studio classroom, I *Let Go* and painted. Suddenly, for the first time in my life, symbols, archetypes, and mythic structures poured through and onto my paintings. Standing back and witnessing the work, I was awestruck at the symbols. There was a transcendent, powerful quality about them. I knew I had found a language I could finally use to share my soul.

What I didn't know is that I had stumbled onto my life's work as well—helping others navigate change by accessing the language of their soul through images and stories.

What I have learned from my own process is the importance of *renewing* my vital energy to have the strength to *Let Go* of what I need to. This was the key to beginning my *Cocoon to Butterfly* process. I needed to *Stop* when I felt "the call."

Rest, refuel, renew, and refresh

I call it the 4R's: Rest, Refuel, *Renew,* and Refresh. Spiritually, the 4R's help us to become *Presence* and experience the quality of love. By opening our hearts, it makes it easier to *Listen* and *Let Go*. There is an opening in our life force field when we take time for *renewal*.

Holding on to old patterns keeps us stuck in a *Cocoon* prison of conditioned energy, preventing us from freely creating our lives. These *Cocoon* prisons are made of dead skin that no longer contains vital aliveness. The life force is gone. There are psychological, ancestral, genetic, cultural, and personality patterns that are ready to drop away if we will only choose to *Stop* and let life naturally unfold.

But one must decide to *Stop*. What would it take for you to give yourself a retreat? For a month, a weekend, a day or an hour?

9. Lisa Longworth

Exercise: Give yourself a retreat

Give yourself the gift of taking a retreat to *Renew* yourself. How long would you now feel comfortable to retreat from daily activities or caring for others to *renew* yourself? Connect with *Nature*—your nature.

Is there a place a few hours' drive from where you live that you could retreat to overnight? Being in solitude is powerful. If possible, take a solo retreat without your significant other or children. Make this your soul's opportunity for *renewal* and the deeper connection to what matters most.

Here are some ideas for retreats:

Take a few minutes off:

1. In the middle of a busy day, take 5 minutes to *Renew* yourself.

2. Change your physical position. If you are sitting in front of a computer, get up and take a break.

3. Connect to *Nature*, for example, a plant or the sky. Breathe. Feel the vital energy replenishing your inner well.

Take an hour off:

1. Make a list of one-hour retreats you can make either at work or at home.

2. Think of places to go that will lift your spirit. Places in *Nature* like a park or even your own backyard are great beginnings.

3. Set a timer for yourself so you don't have to keep checking your watch.

4. Think about an art gallery or art museum. Go to an art supply store, a hardware store, or a second-hand store—not with a specific shopping list, but just to wander around and be inspired.

5. There are probably places you can go in your home for an hour that will give you *renewed* energy. Think about digging in your garden, again with no outcome in mind, but as an opportunity to rest and refuel your energy by connecting with the dirt.

Take off for a 1-3 day retreat:

1. Brainstorm several one-day adventures for your retreat in your own city and write them down. Think about places you don't normally go where you could spend an entire day doing something in a different way that would *Renew* your energy. For instance, you could spend time in *Nature*, have lunch in a nice restaurant, journal, take in the sights, etc.

2. Plan an actual vacation with the purpose of retreat and *renewal*. Do it in such a manner that it supports deep relaxation and inner peace. Going to a resort or spa for health treatments over a few days can be great. Taking a retreat for a creative or spiritual weekend workshop is powerful.

3. Planning a retreat where you can drive in a leisurely manner over one day to get there, one day to be there and one day to return can be a nice retreat adventure. You can start your 3-day adventure by tuning into your intention for the trip. Write it down on a slip of paper or in your journal and then remember to tune into

your intention throughout your trip. Including a symbol for your intention can make it even more powerful. (For example, the intention was "rest" and the symbol was a "sleeping cat.")

Check-in: *Stop & Renew*

Use this check-in to help you develop your signature practice and go deeply into your *transformational* process. Write your answers to the questions in your *C2B Journal* or discuss in your *Cocoon to Butterfly* group.

1. Did you begin your *C2B Journal*? If not, what do you need to do to create one?

2. Did you create a *Cocoon to Butterfly* Sacred Place? If so, what was your experience? If not, how can you do so now?

3. Did you give yourself a retreat? Was your vital energy replenished?

2 BE PRESENT

FOCUS YOUR LENS OF PERCEPTION
MEDITATE & RENEW WITH SILENCE

**"The soul always knows what to do to heal itself.
The challenge is to silence the mind."**

~Carolyn Myss

Strengthen your mental muscles to sustain your attention

If you can refocus your attention, you can *Be Present*. This second change tool is about strengthening your mental muscles to sustain your attention where you want it. This practice of silencing the mental chatter, or meditation, becomes a container to support your growth. Like the egg of a butterfly, to practice meditation creates a spacious container that makes it much easier to see the patterns that no longer serve you. Then as you develop, you can create new patterns that support the life you desire.

Life protects itself as it changes. *Butterfly* eggs have a tough coating, not brittle like that of a bird's egg. The shell is designed to protect the egg from water loss while *allowing* it to breathe. You need a container; a shell for your own changing process, and it also needs to breathe!

Stop automatic patterns to open to what is next

The egg is stationary; it doesn't move while it's gestating into a caterpillar. You also need to *Stop* the daily movement of your automatic patterns to be open to what is next in your life. Imagine that you are in a *Cocoon*; you can't see the world around you because you are inside this *Cocoon* skin, developing into something else. This book is about helping you *Let Go* of the old you and emerging into the authentic *Butterfly* of your own *Becoming*.

Discovering how to hold your unfolding wings

Containers hold things. The butterfly's eggshell holds the developing creature. What will be holding your unfolding wings?

Breath as your tool to come into *Present* awareness

The creative intuitive brain can only be accessed in the *Present* moment. The breath is an essential tool for coming into *Present* awareness. It has been said that if the breathing is at all unsettled, life is not your own. So *Stop* now and focus your attention on your breath. This is meditation. Think of it in its many forms as your container for *transformation*. Like the butterfly's cocoon, this practice will foster the discovery of your authentic path in its stillness.

There are many types of meditation practices, and it will be important for you to discover which one works best for you. Traditional meditation practices often use a mantra, an internal sound or a word that is repeated over and over to bring the mind's attention away from the automatic mental chatter towards silent awareness within. Other meditation practices focus on the breath.

Strengthening your muscles of awareness

Meditation is a mental exercise that strengthens the muscles of awareness. If you haven't meditated, you may not be aware of the distinction between the internal noise of your mind and the silence of simply being *Present*.

When you connect to the silence between your thoughts, the window to your soul opens.

In this chapter, we'll be exploring several creative ways to access our inner silence. Creative meditation practices can include dance, focused time in *Nature*, drawing, music, and other creative processes.

Refocus your attention on the changes you seek

Where our first change tool, *Renew*, refuels our energy for the *transformational* journey, Meditation refocuses our attention to the changes we seek. The power of your attention is enormous.

For some of my clients, when they first begin to access silence, the experience can bring up an inner feeling of emptiness that can be scary. Silence can clear away psychological protection, noise that keeps us safe from scary, deeper feelings that precede change. The next step can be learning how to relax and accept the dreaded feelings, not as wrong or bad, but just as what is. Then the silence can open up a glorious portal into peace and a sense of the eternal happening in the moment.

By refocusing our lens of perception, we perceive a quality of life that was previously clouded. Once we see the truth of what is before us, we can't "unsee it." The truth sets us free.

I was set free in my near-death experience at 19 years old. Right after my brain surgery, I was coming back into consciousness when my mind went silent. Instead of seeing myself from the ceiling of the operating room at Scripps Hospital in La Jolla, I saw the Earth from space and realized I was looking at myself. Incredibly beautiful subtle rivers moved in the space between landmasses. What I saw in images then became sound. There was soft music coming from everything that created a sort of choir. The various sounds harmonized. Everything was connected and fully alive. It was incredibly beautiful. I felt bliss beyond what I had ever felt before. I realized I wasn't so much an individual thing as the spaciousness between all things.

I recognized myself as much larger than my individual self. My larger Self reached into everywhere and at the same time, paradoxically, lived nowhere. When I came back into ordinary consciousness, nothing seemed the same. I could feel the aliveness of everything around me with more clarity. That vital aliveness in my body felt the vitality of all life around me. It was as if a sun was always shining within me, and I felt a burning desire to ignite that living fire in everyone I encountered.

Yet, at 19, I was ill prepared to share my newly discovered sunshine with others. Every attempt to joyfully express my experience with others brought the opposite reaction—darkness, and fear. Friends and loved ones suggested I see a psychiatrist. "I think I understand what you went through," an older close friend said, "Your experience sounds like my first LSD trip." That was the closest I came to having another understand my experience. Over the next few months, I tried to share my experience again and again. My parents did make an appointment for their teenage daughter to see a psychiatrist, who just shook his head when I shared my story. I was getting nowhere but in trouble for expressing the experience, so I *stopped* trying.

A *Cocoon* formed around this experience and my intense passion for sharing it. I didn't know for sure if I was crazy. I knew I needed to heal and grow and strengthen myself. At 19 years old, I needed to find my way in the world. More than anything, I needed to belong to the human race, and I wasn't going to sacrifice that need to express my truth at that time.

University life provided safe sanctuary. So for the next five years, I focused on being as normal as possible. My focus was getting good grades and fitting in. At UC San Diego, my art professor Faith Ringgold, introduced mask making to me. Masks mesmerized me. They became a language to express the *transformation* I had experienced. I cast masks out of handmade paper and made sculptures with mixed media.

This sculpture expresses three states of consciousness. The bottom mask represents the unconscious. The branches on the bottom of the mask are roots connecting it to the earth and all that is unconscious.

The middle mask is our self-conscious or ego self, our inner mind chatter that tells us who we are. This mask has roots connecting it to the unconscious mask also splitting open as it experiences silence. The self-conscious mask opens up in meditation to a higher consciousness, ascending with wings to a golden radiance. Constructing this sculpture when I was 25 years old helped me claim my truth and communicate my experience, but I still had far to go to get out of my stuck *Cocoon*.

10. Lisa Longworth

Beauty as meditation

Simply being *Present* with the beauty of life is a meditation in and of itself. Beauty *Stops* the mind. I find going out into my garden and sitting in *Nature* can dramatically shift my awareness. Sometimes, I will close my eyes in silence, focusing on my breathing and the space between my thoughts. The benefits of traditional closed-eye meditation are worth their weight in gold. However, *Nature's* beauty in my garden, absorbing the presence of trees, flowers and hummingbirds *Stops* my mind immediately and is so pleasurable.

In meditation, spaciousness opens between you and your mindstream (your thoughts). It is easier to be aware that you are not your thoughts; you have thoughts, but they are not who you are. Then after meditation, unless one is enlightened, we usually connect to our thoughts again as if they are our true inner voice, an expression of our essential self. We are automatically absorbed into focusing on our thinking until we witness the mindstream and choose to refocus on resting in the silent presence deep within our heart and soul.

Then life changes. Sometimes, life patterns are changed dramatically by circumstance. Big losses can trigger change and force one into a transition. Often, clients come into my office due to the loss of a marriage or a job. Suddenly their roles disappear and the questions arise, "who am I now, and where am I going?"

Martha, a soft-featured 58-year-old brunette, came into my office experiencing waves of anxiety after retiring as a high school administrator. She seemed to be vacillating between short joyful moments of freedom and long, scary episodes of dread at the unscheduled time in her days.

Her *Cocoon to Butterfly* drawing showed her challenge as a small and black box with bars on it that was on the bottom of the page. It was titled "Jailed Joy." Her *Butterfly* drawing had large free and open circles. She spontaneously named her *Butterfly* drawing "Dancing" and recalled an experience from her 5-year-old self.

"It was a warm late spring day in Missouri on the small farm where I grew up. I was out in the garden. I remember flowers everywhere. I felt so delighted that I took off all my clothes and danced in the garden. My mother came out and screamed at me. I was overtaken by terror. I grabbed my clothes and ran into the house and into my room. She punished me harshly for being such a bad girl. I felt such shame, yet I'll never forget the joy I felt dancing naked in my garden. I don't think I have felt that kind of freedom since then."

We focused on Martha reclaiming moments of that kind of freedom through a meditation process that involved

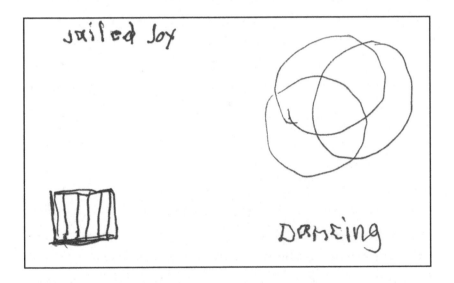

beauty. Traditional closed-eye meditation was difficult for Martha; however, she found an instant connection to silence in her garden. Her 1928 cottage had a very private backyard with large old trees. There was a pair of

Prairiefire Crabapple trees that were ablaze in cranberry-colored flowers this time of year.

She created her practice twice a day; in the morning she would bring her breakfast to the outside backyard. Mindfully, she would slowly eat and focus on the beauty around her. In the afternoon at 3 pm, Martha listened to a favorite song and slowly danced with the plants around her.

She reported in her next session that the afternoon dance in the garden was difficult. *Listening* to the music helped, but she still felt stuck. When we started our work together, she had three possible "theme songs" for her *Cocoon to Butterfly* journey. But Irene Cara's "Flashdance... What a Feeling" caused Martha to experience a consistent overwhelming exuberance. She downloaded the song to her Samsung smartphone and began using it with her daily practices.

When we talked about what Martha was experiencing when she felt stuck, her forehead wrinkled up. "My thoughts about being bad overwhelm me. Instead of dancing, I want to roll up into a little ball." My suggestion was for her to consciously shift her attention from her thinking mind to the still quiet place inside her heart. I introduced an exercise, *"Entering Presence"* (See page 58). We practiced it in my office. Martha reported back that it was working well. When the terrible dark storm of thoughts would arise when she was dancing, she would refocus her attention to her quiet place within her heart. "It's an amazing meditation for me. Although I first started doing it in the garden while dancing, at your suggestion, now I use it anytime my thinking mind has my attention and is bringing me down. Even while driving, when my thinking is making me anxious, I just bring my focus into that inner place that is always calm and silent. Those nasty trouble-making thoughts instantly lose their charge and disappear. All I feel is peace and stillness. I am in my "Dancing" *Butterfly Self* then, most definitely. My stuck place, "Jailed Joy," clearly exists when I am stuck in the prison of my thinking, rather than when I am in the silent freedom of my being."

"Meditation is not a way of making your mind quiet. It's a way of entering into the quiet that's already there—buried under the 50,000 thoughts the average person thinks every day."

~Deepak Chopra

Exercise: Entering presence

"Entering the quiet that's already there," as Deepak Chopra puts it, is the focus of our next exercise. It is about paying attention in a particular way in the *Present* moment without judgment. By simply observing the stream of events inside and outside, we become creatively detached and enter presence. Something powerful happens when we can perceive our mind and our body objectively. We observe our actions without praise or blame. Developing the ability to enter presence can greatly assist us in disregarding old dramas. We can *Stop* and watch the movie rather than be consumed by it. We become aware of the choice we have to fully engage with our thoughts or feelings, or choose something else.

1. Witness yourself. Watch yourself, your thoughts, and become aware of your breath. You may witness yourself caught in mind chatter or a story that you are telling yourself about someone or something. Or you may

witness a challenging emotion that may be deeper than the mind chatter. Simply witness it without naming it or trying to change it.

2. Relax your mind, body, and soul and enter into your quiet place—into the deep center core of your heart.

3. Effortlessly abide in this silent presence; this is your deepest true self. This quiet is always there.

Cultivate abiding in this quiet place within you—always there, always your essential self. It is eternal, authentic, peaceful, and loving. Come home here whenever you feel lost or confused. Cultivate presence.

11. Lisa Longworth

Exercise: Your place of peace meditation

This is a basic meditation that can be used alone or as a "base camp" to then climb higher to creative consciousness with other exercises in this book.

1. Sit with your spine erect and your feet on the ground. Close your eyes and become conscious of your breath.

2. Feel a stream of energy moving from your heart to your head. Then feel or see it connecting with everything above you until you reach the sun. Then return to your heart and feel or see that same stream of energy moving down into the ground through your feet until it reaches the core of the earth. Continue to breathe and experience this vital stream of energy moving through your heart up to the sun and then down to the earth.

3. Now, continuing to breathe deeply, you are going to travel to Your Place of Peace. You might find yourself at the seashore, a mountain stream, on an island or in the desert. This will be a place where you feel safe, loved, and connected to the beauty of *Nature*. Go there now.

4. In your imagination with your eyes closed, look around you. See the colors, shapes, objects and natural world around you. Feel the ground beneath your feet as you are seated. Now take

your time and smell the air around you. Then savor the tastes in your mouth. Continue to breathe deeply. Now *Listen* to the sounds of your environment. Put your full attention on what you hear.

5. Fully take in Your Place of Peace for as long as you like. You can come back here anytime you wish.

6. You can also use this meditation, or self-guided visualization, as a process to put you in a deeper state of awareness to start another exercise.

7. Your Place of Peace meditation can be done anytime and anywhere. Anytime you feel you have lost your peace, such as in line at a grocery store, in traffic, in the middle of an irritating experience, try accessing Your Place of Peace. You don't need to close your eyes to get great benefit. If you've done this exercise deeply and fully a half a dozen times or more, it will make it much easier to do it on the "run."

"The quieter you become, the more you can hear."

~Thich Nhat Hahn

Exercise: *Butterfly Breathing*

To clear your mind and cleanse your lens of perception

Your breath is one of the most powerful tools you can use to refocus your attention away from automatic thinking to *Listen* to your deeper self. Here is a breathing meditation to support the release of mental and emotional energy. It will help to clear your mind and is good for your health in general. You can do it anywhere and anytime. I have done it discreetly while waiting in an airport for my plane, as well as in the morning and evening in my favorite chair at home.

You will focus your attention on your breath, breathing through your nose and keeping your mouth closed and relaxed. You will close your eyes and slowly breathe in, letting your belly be soft and filled with air in a relaxed and easy way. When it naturally reaches its limit and the breath is full, without pause, you will release your breath through your nose.

You will continually breathe without pauses between breaths. It is best to do this exercise while sitting in a chair with your hands on your thighs, palms open towards the sky.

You will use your fingers to count the incoming breaths. Starting with either hand, you will let your thumb rise first. Then, each time you inhale, you will lift a finger. After you do this exercise for a while, lifting your fingers becomes automatic; however, it may take a few tries at counting with your fingers until it becomes effortless.

Try the finger counting exercise right now.

1. Start with your right hand, palm facing up and hand relaxed and open. As you breathe out, let your thumb lift up, keeping your palm relaxed. This is your first in and out breath.

2. With the next outgoing breath, let your pointing finger rise and, with ease, touch the thumb that is already up. The touch between the first finger and thumb is very light and natural.

3. With the third in and out breath, you will let the middle finger effortlessly rise to touch the thumb.

4. Next, with the fourth breath, the ring finger will rise to touch the thumb.

5. Lastly, the little finger will follow with the next breath.

6. Now all fingers on your right hand are gently touching each other. All the fingers don't need to be in contact with the thumb, they just need to be gently connected to each other.

7. Leave the right hand with all fingers gently risen and start counting breaths with your left hand.

8. Following the same process you just did with your right hand, let your left thumb rise with the next exhale and so forth until all your fingers on your left hand have risen and are gently touching each other.

9. With your next breath, gently release all ten fingers so that both palms are open again, as they were in the beginning.

10. Begin the same process all over again, until you feel like you are finished.

With *Butterfly Breathing*, you will feel two things going on: the breath rising and falling, and your fingers slightly rising, connecting with each other, and falling open again (after ten breaths).

I call this meditation exercise *"Butterfly Breathing"* because the rising and falling of the fingers look like a butterfly's wings as it rests on a flower, opening, and closing.

You can also imagine your lungs as butterfly wings opening and closing, if this is helpful for you. Try following my directions as closely as possible for several sittings, and then make your adjustments. The key is to work creatively with your continuous breathing and gentle finger movements with ease and experimentation.

Freedom meditation

Some meditation practices focus on a mantra, an internal sound or word that is repeated over and over again. This practice uses self-inquiry or four questions to still the mind. It can be done anytime and anywhere in a busy life.

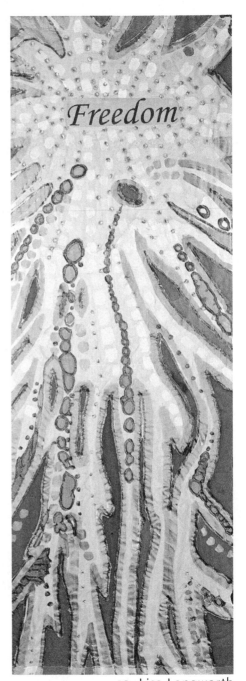

Freedom

12. Lisa Longworth

1. **Intention:**

   When you are aware you have become trapped in thought, ask yourself:

   What is my intention? Then pause. You will naturally go into silence and your mind will become quiet. *Listen* for the first response that arises. This response is your intention.

   Example: Imagine you are taking a walk on the beach to clear your mind. Instead, you find yourself thinking about all of the other things you need to do. The moment you become aware of this, ask yourself, "Intention?' Or more fully, ask yourself, "What is my intention?" Pause and wait for an answer to arise in your mind. Perhaps you hear "relax" or "my intention is to relax."

2. **Attention:**

   Where do I need to put my attention?

The next question you ask yourself is "Where do I put my attention?" Or simply ask, "Attention?" Then pause. In the silence, *Listen* for the first response. This response answers where you need to put your attention.

Example: As you are walking on the beach, your thoughts have taken you away from the moment. You have asked yourself already about your intention and received the answer "relax." Now you ask yourself, "Where do I put my attention?" pausing to *Listen* to the answer you have received, "put your attention on your breath." Now you focus on your breath moving in and out of your nostrils as you walk on the beach.

3. Action:

What action do I need to take?

The third question you ask yourself, after "intention" and "attention" is "What action do I need to take?" or "Action?" Pause to wait for the answer within you. Then take that action.

Example: You are walking on the beach and have asked yourself "intention" and received "relax," then "attention" and received "breath," and then you ask the third question, "What action do I need to take?" The answer that comes to you is "press my thumb and forefinger together as I breathe." So now you walk with the intention to relax, your attention on your breath and the action of touching your thumb and forefinger together as you walk.

4. Gratitude:

What am I grateful for?

As you ask yourself the last question, "What am I grateful for?" *Allow* your mind to fill in the answers. Since often mind chatter can be strongest when we feel we are a victim of our circumstance, it is impossible to be in victimhood and grateful at the same time.

Example: You are walking on the beach and have asked yourself "intention" and received "relax", then "attention" and received "breath", and then you ask the third question, "Action?" and received touching your fingers together as you walk. Then you ask, "What am I grateful for?" and your thoughts are "for my family, my health, my time off right now to walk on the beach."

Over a decade ago, while walking on the Cardiff

Beach in San Diego in the late afternoon, these four questions spontaneously came to me as an antidote for my distracted busy mind. Since then, I find this Four Question practice powerful for a mindful life. After sitting for 20 minutes in traditional closed-eye sitting meditation, the mind is so clean and relaxed. The problem today is our busy lifestyles often make this practice outdated and difficult to achieve. This meditation can be done in 10 seconds or 2 minutes, while driving a car, in a meeting or while making love. It can be done again and again, as needed. It instantly brings you back to the moment when your mind *Stops* to ponder the question. And you also access your creativity in answering the questions, often directly from your intuition. In the light of the question, *you unlock the prison of your mind and it becomes a prism to let a rainbow of possibilities shine through.*

Signature Practice

Check-in: *Be Present & Meditate*

Use this check-in to help you develop your signature practice and go deeply into your *transformational* process. Write your answers to the questions in your *C2B Journal* or discuss in your *Cocoon to Butterfly* group.

1. How are you using your *C2B Journal* as part of your signature practice?

2. Which meditation exercises did you try? Which ones do you want to incorporate into daily life?

3. Have you received any new insight from incorporating meditation into your daily life?

4. Did you put anything new in your *Cocoon to Butterfly* Sacred Place?

Did you know?

After hatching, most caterpillars eat their egg case as their first meal. The second meal comes from the plant where the egg was laid. Mother butterfly is smart; her baby caterpillar does not have to hunt very far for food. The caterpillar grows very quickly as it eats constantly.

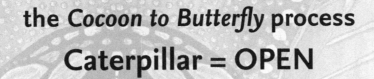

the *Cocoon to Butterfly* process
Caterpillar = OPEN

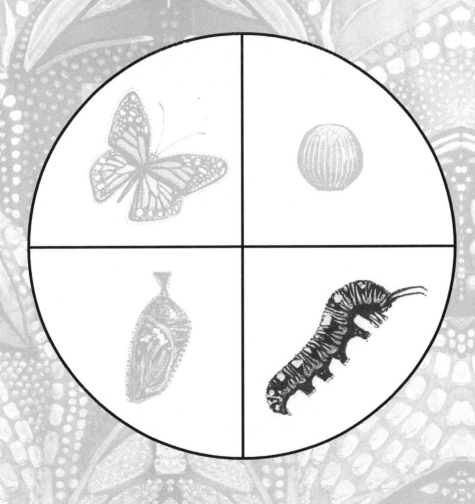

caterpillar

Nourish yourself with listening to images, intuition and creative tension

In this part of our metamorphosis, we nourish ourselves by *eating* Nature *and drinking beauty,* to receive the vital energy necessary to feed our essential nature and make the changes we seek.

3 OPEN

In the natural alchemy of the butterfly's change process, a caterpillar is an eating machine, nourishing itself to grow and change. This mirrors our inner *transformational* process to nourish ourselves by listening to our intuition through our guiding images.

4 ALLOW

Once our essential nature is acknowledged and nourished, it moves on its own, like a river. This river flows with vital energy or authentic life force. *Allowing* it to be uncomfortable, we then let the creative tension or stress of change exist without resisting it. Then we are out of our own way, released from our inner prison and life flows effortlessly.

3 OPEN

ALIGN WITH INNER SEEING AND INNER LISTENING
NOURISH WITH IMAGES AND INTUITION

**"There is a voice
that doesn't use
words, listen."**

~Rumi

A different kind of listening

Listening to the "voice that doesn't use words," is what this chapter is about. We are not talking about listening to voices outside of ourselves, such as listening to others talk. The voice we are to *Listen* to is our intuition, metaphors, symbols and stories. We are to *Listen* to our images of change and the stories they tell us by listening to our intuition. It's INNER listening.

Your intuition, metaphors, symbols, and stories

The problem today is that we aren't taught to *Listen* deeply to ourselves—to *Listen* to our hearts and souls. Our culture teaches us to perform, achieve and produce. This force dominates the first half of our lives. As passive recipients of our culture, we take in so much without discernment.

Our own perception becomes clouded with concepts and beliefs that block our ability to see clearly. I love the way Anais Nin puts it, "We don't see things as they are, we see things as we are." We need fresh eyes to see the world and *Listen* to our deepest truth.

Metaphors, symbols, and personal stories are powerful ways to *Listen* to deeper meaning. They express universal truths in a non-verbal language. Like Rumi's quote in the beginning of this chapter, "there is a voice that doesn't use words, listen," learning to *Listen* to our intuition that speaks through the symbolic realm can give us a royal road to our authentic path.

Our brain is hardwired to love visualizations. Almost 50% of our brain is involved in visual processing and 70% of all of our sensory receptors are in our eyes. In less than 1/10th of a second we get a visual scene. In our daily lives, we are receiving information all the time in our surroundings. Our minds often process that information verbally through our inner dialogue in our thinking process.

Our modern use of emojis on our cell phones comes from an age-old tradition of communicating with pictures that go back to hieroglyphics over 5,000 years ago. We communicate with ourselves through our *Cocoon to Butterfly* pictures—our very personal images of change.

Listening to your images of change

To connect with what matters most in our lives, we must learn the skill of deep listening. Deep listening involves attending closely to our essential core self and receiving the messages. How do you *Listen* to yourself? Do you trust your feelings and have access to your intuition? Often we lose our deeper connection to this listening as children when it becomes necessary to fit into the world. To survive, we need the love and approval of our parents and authorities. We go to school and are taught to perform, to achieve and to produce. We get good grades in school by following the rules and doing what we are told. We find work in the world by making a living and performing as we are supposed to. We follow the rules of our culture and find a mate, make a house and have children.

Suddenly stuck in your invisible prison

Then suddenly everything can change. We no longer feel fulfilled or happy. Something definitely is not right, and we don't have a clue what it is. We are stuck in the *Cocoon* of our past patterns and conditioning. Unconscious old patterns are invisible prisons. In our stuckness, we continually bump into the invisible bars of our prisons and don't know where the doors are. Our unique inner images give us keys to unlock our doors and find our freedom from inside out.

Receiving messages from your deep listening

The invisible prison of my client, Mattie Simmons, had kept her working diligently as an executive assistant for a high-level CEO until her ex-husband suggested passionately she work with me. Mattie was a strikingly beautiful blond, blue-eyed woman in her late 40's. Mattie had been trained well by her mother and society to serve others, especially men who were in roles of power. She also had a level of beauty and power combined with a sharp mind that gave her an open door to rise in the corporate world as an assistant. Yet her soul felt depleted in the work. She was sick of the corporate game of serving egocentric men who were focused on bottom line profits. Mattie craved to feel alive and connected to something deeper.

Her ex-husband, Dave, had worked with me for a few years before he recommended Mattie to come and see me. Dave

"Until you make the unconscious conscious, it will direct your life and you will call it fate."

~C.G Jung

witnessed a fire light up in Mattie when she created a goddess collage from magazine photos in a workshop. He urged that she support this creative opening by working with a professional who could encourage her to continue to develop this aspect of herself.

In our first session, her *Cocoon to Butterfly* drawing revealed two images. Her *Cocoon* drawing was a tightly tangled knot she entitled "Stuck," and her *Butterfly* drawing was an illuminated goddess figure called *"Listening."* In talking about her first drawing, she told me that the older she became, the tighter the box became, and now it was suffocating her. She felt stuck without a way to escape her box.

Her *Butterfly* drawing spoke to her in a powerful way. Her lips trembled as she spoke. "To be free, you must *Listen* to me" she exclaimed, beaming brightly as she had become the image itself and spoke its wisdom to me. Then the next thing out of Mattie's mouth was, "I have no idea how to do this."

Over the next few months, we created her "*Listening* to Goddess" curriculum. Mattie developed new patterns in her life. In the evening after work, instead of watching TV for several hours, she went into her den and poured through old magazines. She tore out images that called to her: a lavender rose, huge red raspberry, a young woman's lips and a bowl of fresh fruit. Then she carefully cut out each image and assemble them into a whole goddess figure.

Carving out time on a regular basis to make art was empowering in her life. The process called her to *Listen* to a deep wisdom inside of herself. It evoked beauty and truth—a creative spiritual connection directly through her veins as she gave herself the gift of creating art. Within a few months, a body of goddess images had been born from Mattie's daily practice that would guide her over the next years to leave corporate America to start her own company. She had found her voice by listening to spontaneously created images and found the courage to walk away from her past.

Over the years of working with thousands of individuals using images to navigate change, I continue to be in awe of their power to cut through the fog of mental confusion and layers of conditioning from the past.

> "Not until we tell ourselves a story can we make sense of our experience."
>
> ~Jerome Bruner

Exercise: *Cocoon to Butterfly* drawing process

Requires: 30-60 minutes of uninterrupted time, writing paper and pen, felt pen or colored pencils, two pieces of paper folded vertically. The paper size should be a minimum of 8 X 10" or maximum size of 10 X 16".

Try using either a clock or your cell phone timer. There will be four timed sessions of 2-10 minutes each. You must do the whole exercise including both drawings and after that naming them, and finally writing about your *Cocoon and Butterfly Self.*

Writing Process

Start with your writing paper and take 5 minutes to answer both of the following questions. You may want to internally repeat the question to yourself while closing your eyes before you start writing.

1. What is the change you are going through? What is your biggest challenge right now? If you feel stuck or frustrated with your situation, how would you describe it? What do you need to *Let Go* of? We use the symbolism of the

Cocoon to mirror our stuck place. What does your *Cocoon* look like? How does it feel? (Allow 5 minutes)

2. Now shifting gears, where do you want to go in your change process? What is your desired outcome? If you were to break through your stuck *Cocoon* place, imagine what it might look like to be the *Butterfly* of your own *Becoming*. (Allow 5 minutes)

3. Reread your writing and underline any words that jump out at you. Pause for a moment after you've done this to be with yourself and the process. (2-3 minutes)

Drawing process

Get out your unlined paper, pens, and pencils. If you have a large piece of paper, fold it in half so you have two portraits (long way) pages to draw on. This is a scribble drawing, not art making. Create these drawings quickly and spontaneously without thinking about it very much. Over the years of doing this exercise, it seems those who make a quick visual expression with little art-making energy expressed have the best "art medicine" to work with.

If you have an art background, this exercise can be more difficult than if you don't have that experience. Our intention is to let energy out on the page, not create something visually beautiful. Imagine you are four years old and scribbling just for the fun of it.

1. **Draw the *Cocoon* on the left side.**

   (2 to 3 minutes on this side) This is on the left side of a large folded paper or on a single piece of paper. You have already written about your challenges, frustrations and places where you feel stuck. Now you are going to quickly scribble an expression of this energy sticking to your 3-minute timeline. Again, we are not making art or anything beautiful, just getting raw energy out on the page.

2. **Draw the *Butterfly* on the right side.**

   (2 to 3 minutes on this side) This drawing is done on the right side of the paper or on a single piece of paper. You have already written about your *Butterfly* to bring the deeper energies of it to the surface. Now you are going to draw what it would look like to emerge from your stuck *Cocoon* and become the *Butterfly* of your own *Becoming*.

Name each drawing. (1 minute) First look at your *Cocoon* drawing. Let it (the images) tell you its name. Breathe and *Listen*. It could be a single word or a phrase with several words. Whatever first comes to you is perfect; don't second-guess it, even if it doesn't make sense. Write it down on the bottom of the page of your *Cocoon* drawing. Then *Listen* to the *Butterfly* side and write down the title for this side.

Let your *Cocoon to Butterfly* drawing talk to you.
(15-30 minutes) Now that you've created your drawings, it will be helpful to gain insight from them.

1. Part One: (5 minutes each side) You will *Listen* to your *Cocoon* drawing first and then your *Butterfly* drawing, imagining there was someone in front of you looking at your drawing. You will tell them a story about it including your ideas and imaginings about various aspects of it.

2. Part Two: (5-10 minutes in total) Now you will write again, pulling out any more insights and awareness from either side or the tension created by both drawings. Include any intuitive guidance or new ideas that emerge spontaneously.

Exercise: Non-dominant hand writing

Using the hand we don't normally write with in our journal process can be a powerful tool to *Listen* to the wisdom stored in our bodies. By doing so, we *Allow* the unconscious to speak through images or written words. Emotions that have been stuffed into the body begin to reveal themselves.

When you are feeling stuck with something in your life, and you can't seem to get clear, try writing about it in your *C2B Journal.*

1. Sit quietly and tune into your body. Close your eyes. *Meditate* by focusing your attention on your feet and slowly move upward until you reach the top of your head. Notice any areas of your body that feel painful or out of balance.

2. Draw a simple outline of your body and use markers to color areas where there is pain or discomfort. Or instead of a body, if something else calls to be drawn, draw that.

3. Interview the drawing by writing the following questions with your dominant hand. Then write the response with your non-dominant hand.

Questions:

A. What or who are you? (Write with dominant hand) (Respond with the non-dominant hand.)

B. Tell me how you feel? (Write with dominant hand) (Respond with the non-dominant hand.)

C. Why? (Write with dominant hand) (Respond with the non-dominant hand.)

D. Tell me how I can help? (Write with dominant hand) (Respond with the non-dominant hand.)

An excellent book for more information on non-dominant hand writing is Lucia Capacchoine's *The Power of Your Other Hand.*

Exercise: Your genius council

This exercise will access your inner wisdom, quiet your mind through meditation, and develop your ability to *Listen* to your intuition. Begin by taking 5 minutes to *Meditate* in a quiet place with your body in a relaxed position. Then *Allow* yourself to follow this guided meditation.

Visualize yourself in the future, perhaps 100 years or more. There is an elevator in front of you that will take you to the 1000th floor, where you visit the Diamond Dome. See yourself entering the elevator and pressing the button to the 1000th floor. When you arrive there, you walk down a long corridor and then up a white winding staircase to then enter the Diamond Dome. This large rounded room has a huge clear faceted crystal dome with a large round table with seven chairs under it.

As you look up to the ceiling, it is as if you are inside of a diamond, the facets reflect the exact pattern of a diamond seen from the inside. Witness the triangular facets and see the millions of sparkling stars of the Universe outside.

Now look at the large round table in front of you. See the seven chairs. Notice that one has been pulled back from the table and sit in it. The six remaining chairs are empty.

You realize that you are there to call in your council of Master Geniuses that are available throughout history to serve your highest quest in your life. You will quietly invite them into council by asking yourself first:

1. "What is my highest intention in this lifetime?"

Then wait for the answer to pop into your mind. Simply focus on it as it becomes crystal clear in your mind. For instance, the answer might be, "to serve in the evolution of humanity." With this quest in mind, then ask for guidance from the Collective Master Genius Council to further your understanding.

You will now witness each chair being filled by one Genius in history who can help you (i.e. Buddha, Jesus, Einstein, Gandhi, or a family member). You may see all six that drop into the chairs or perhaps one or a few will be seen this time. You are gathering your Master Genius Council. *Allow* whatever happens to be perfect.

In silence, meet your council member or members. It doesn't matter if only one or many are assembled. They may flash in and out of form, or take only partial form. Whatever happens in the *Present* moment is perfect. You may hear them rather than see them. This is perfect as well. Take a minute to simply be with whatever is showing up now.

Now ask your Council for their guidance with your life or life circumstance. Let the members speak. In the center of the table, a holographic movie may appear revealing the situation, the characters, and unfolding drama for you to see it clearly. A council member may have a gift to give you that could be a symbol that you will understand more fully after this council meeting. Receive whatever is given to you now. Be with the gifts for a moment to fully take them into your awareness.

Then ask this question to the council:

2. "Where do I need to put my attention?"

Listen to the answer in whatever form it may come to you and take a moment to absorb it. Then ask:

3. "What action do I take now?"

Receive the communication and take a moment to absorb the answer. Then ask yourself:

4. "What am I grateful for?"

You will share what arises in your heart back to your council members. You could express your gratitude. For instance, "thank you for the opportunity to be an instrument of good energy on Earth. I am grateful for my perfect life and to serve in helping others have the same. Thank you Life for this opportunity."

After you share your gratitude, then the Diamond Dome Master Genius Council meeting ends. Watch how your members dissolve form and return home. Then witness the empty chairs. This will indicate you are ready to leave the Dome. Exit the round room, return to the elevator, take the elevator to the first floor and exit the building.

If you are inspired, write about your experience in your journal. The important information will be the answers from your meditation questions.

1. Did any new Intention come through?

2. Where now does your Attention need to go?

3. What Action now needs to be taken?

4. In expressing your Gratitude, is there anything to note now?

5. Do you have any new symbols to add to your *Cocoon to Butterfly* sacred space?

6. Consider playing with your creativity and making something from your new images.

If you have a recording device, consider recording yourself reading the instructions so that you can relax while completing this meditaion. Or you can write down the essential steps in your own words if that helps you remember the process.

Check-In: *Open & Listen*

Use this check-in to help you develop your signature practice and go deeply into your *transformational* process. Write your answers to the questions in your *C2B Journal* or discuss in your *Cocoon to Butterfly* group.

1. How did your *Cocoon to Butterfly* drawings come out? If you haven't drawn them yet, what's holding you back?

2. What stories came from your drawings?

3. Did you experiment with the Non-dominant Hand Writing exercise?

4. Did you access your inner wisdom with the Genius Council? What were some of the insights you gained?

"Part of doing something is listening. We are listening. To the sun. To the stars. To the wind."

~Madeleine L'Englc, *Swiftly Tilting Planet*

"The word 'listen' contains the same letters as the word 'silent'."

~Alfred Brendel

"You know, I have come to think listening is love, that's what it really is."

~Brenda Ueland

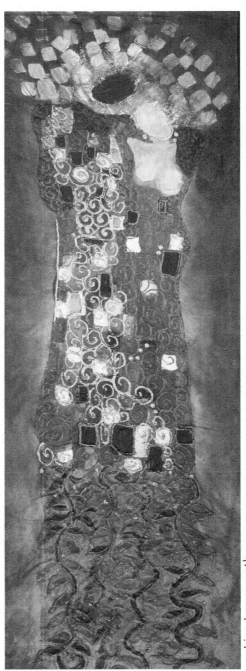

13. Lisa Longworth

4 ALLOW

EMBRACE DISCOMFORT
ALLOW CREATIVE TENSION

"I've been absolutely terrified every moment
of my life and I've never let it keep me from
doing a single thing that I wanted to do."

-Georgia O'Keeffe

"To live a creative life,
we must lose our fear
of being wrong."

~Joseph Chilton Pearce

Allowing your creative tension to exist

It may seem natural to react and pull away when a
situation feels uncomfortable and unsafe. We are
genetically programed to move towards that which

feels good. Yet, in the creative process of becoming our highest self, we must *Allow* creative tension to exist as we go through our metamorphosis. The alchemical process of this caterpillar phase of the butterfly's lifecycle calls us to feel the tension or stress of change without resisting it.

The great thing about this uncomfortable tension is that *Nature* seeks to resolve it. If you can *Allow* it to exist without resisting it, it naturally moves you forward. I love the way Robert Fritz talks about this in his book, *Creating*:

> *A basic principle found throughout* Nature *is this: Tension seeks resolution... During the creative process, you have an eye on where you want to go, and you also have an eye on where you currently are. There will always be structural tension in the beginning of the creative process, for there will always be a discrepancy between what you want and what you have.*

As you ascend to higher levels of development, the creative process will challenge you. Sometimes, you may experience thoughts and feelings that are uncomfortable and stressful. It is easy to run away from them when they come. Our instincts tell us something is wrong. We are wrong, this is the wrong path for us, and we don't have what it takes to stay on course. However, creative tension is inherent in a creative life. If you want to be fully alive, learn to live with the tension.

The tension is like a rubber band between the *Butterfly* of your own *Becoming* and the old skin of the *Cocoon* that needs to be shed for the butterfly to emerge. The *Butterfly* of your own *Becoming* is your vision and the *Cocoon* is your current reality. The tension between where you are now and where you want to be is the creative tension.

Your creative tension is a natural phenomenon

Sometimes we experience confusion around our ideas of happiness and advanced spirituality. The fantasy often is that we can attain these higher states and then should not feel tension or discomfort in our daily life. However, if you are committed to creating and manifesting your visions, creative tension will show up, and you may feel some discomfort. **It is just easier if you can recognize the creative tension as natural phenomena of the creative process versus an unresolved psychological problem you have.** The discomfort still could be an unresolved issue, AND the discomfort in the creative tension IS A PART of the nature of change. The creative tension between what is here now and our vision of what we want is a powerful dynamic that doesn't feel all happy and all peaceful. It is challenging, difficult at times and often can feel fierce rather than passive or peaceful.

Samantha Smith, a bright executive in her late 30's, desperately wanted a child. Her dating process was as she put it, "disastrous." Climbing the corporate ladder was easy compared with her search for a husband. The *Butterfly* drawing she created had a kite flying in an open blue sky. Her *Cocoon* drawing was a dense ball of energy entitled "Trapped." The story of her drawings went like this: "In the world of romantic love, the harder I work, the tighter this black box becomes."

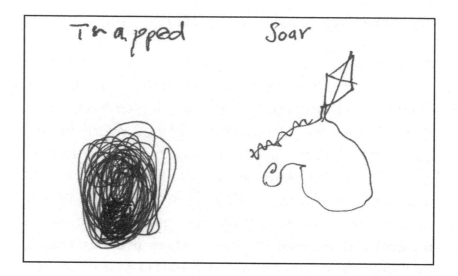

In the six months Samantha was in her *Cocoon to Butterfly* group, she got feedback from other members that helped her deal with her uncomfortable "Trapped" feelings. When the group got to this chapter, Samantha felt as if it had been written for her. "I will *Allow* it to be uncomfortable," she would tell herself again and again. The *Butterfly* of her own *Becoming*, she was discovering, was more about her connection to life than finding a husband. "When I am connected, I naturally soar! With or without a man, it doesn't matter, as long as I am true to myself." Samantha was accepting her life as it is.

Your mentor can provide affirmation and guidance

Sometimes, creative tension can best resolve itself when someone else can truly see us. Have you heard that idea, "when the student is ready, the teacher appears?" Mentors can provide affirmation and guidance to help us trust our unique way of connecting to what matters most. We need to be seen and heard by someone who truly can receive us—someone who sees our gifts and encourages us to flower. It is affirming to have someone you admire and trust see you and support your life in authentically unfolding.

Dr. Jonas Salk was one of my most significant mentors. He showed up during a very challenging transitional time where I was struggling to find my true calling in life. I had graduated with a bachelor's degree completing my own special project, "Symbols, Rituals and *Transformation*," that dealt with my near-death experience through a large performance art event. Although it was healing to successfully share the experience I had *Cocooned* for five years, I felt lost and confused as to the next step to take after graduation. Then I met Jonas Salk.

Dr. Salk came to a charity event at my oceanfront home in La Jolla, and we instantly connected. Curiously, I was born the year his Salk Institute for Biological Studies was established in La Jolla. He discovered one of the first successful polio vaccines. Twenty-five years after he created the institute, he had a vision of a Creativity Institute to bring creative geniuses from all disciplines to solve world problems, not by traditional means but by a creative approach.

We communicated primarily by phone, sharing almost daily dialogues on creativity and intuition for five years. So many times, I would hear him say,

"Let intuition be your guide, with reason by its side."

One day I was in my garden talking with Jonas. I hoped he could tell me what to do. As I waited for his reply, a yellow butterfly landed on the back of my hand. The world *Stopped* and lit up in that moment. In the silence, I heard, *"Cocoon to Butterfly."* The next day a woman named Sarah called me. She spoke about how stuck she felt and how ready she was to break free. "Like a *Cocoon to Butterfly*?" I asked. "Oh my God, yes! Can you help me find my wings?" she replied. And so it went, like a bee to a flower, people were drawn to me to help them heal. And my own heart started to heal. I enrolled in a graduate program for psychology. My *Cocoon to Butterfly* practice grew.

Exercise: Mentoring

As artists of encouragement, mentors can be spiritual guides. They have the ability to see and summon the gifts of those they work with. Mentoring comes from a Greek concept that is over 3,500 years old. In Homer's *Odyssey*, Telemachus, the son of Odysseus, had a mentor. He was asked to watch over the development of his son. The word mentor means "wise counselor" or "guide."

1. Throughout history, if you could summon the ultimate mentor for yourself who would it be and why? Write the response in your *C2B Journal*.

2. If you would like a real life mentor, write about the qualities you are looking for in that person. What do you want to get out of the relationship and how do you want to be guided?

3. Read biographies of the kind of person that would be your ideal mentor.

4. Make a strong intention to bring your mentor into your life and watch it happen!

Exercise: Witnessing consciousness

Develop the witness within you to become a neutral observer of your life for more clarity and peace of mind. This exercise will help you notice the feelings of tension or stress and bring curiosity rather than judgment to them.

1. *Stop* and simply be with whatever is happening in the moment. You stub your toe and it hurts. In silence and stillness, simply be with the situation, watch and feel it, *allowing* there to be no internal commentary. Then when the mindstream of thoughts return, see if you can have an unimpassioned reaction to them.

2. Cultivate your internal muscles to witness life. Even 10 seconds of silence and witnessing can *Allow* you more spaciousness and freedom to see clearly.

3. In awakening witness consciousness, you cultivate detached self-observation. This is a powerful spiritual tool to evolve into a life of higher awareness.

Check-In: *Allow*

Use this check-in to help you develop your signature practice and go deeply into your *transformational* process. Write your answers to the questions in your *C2B Journal* or discuss in your *Cocoon to Butterfly* group.

1. Can you relate to creative tension? Have you experienced it and then *allowed* it to be there without judgment or resistance?

2. Do you have a mentor now? Would you like one? Did you do the mentoring exercise?

3. What was your experience with the Witnessing Consciousness exercise?

4. How is your signature practice evolving? Are you writing in your *C2B Journal*? Which meditation exercises are resonating for you?

Did you know?

The butterfly's cocoon is called a chrysalis coming from the Greek word for gold. In its profound metamorphosis, the caterpillar's body digests itself from the inside out becoming a kind of soup. Then the imaginal cells, the future cells of the butterfly, eat the caterpillar soup in this radical *transformation* that becomes an adult butterfly.

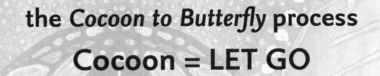

the *Cocoon to Butterfly* process

Cocoon = LET GO

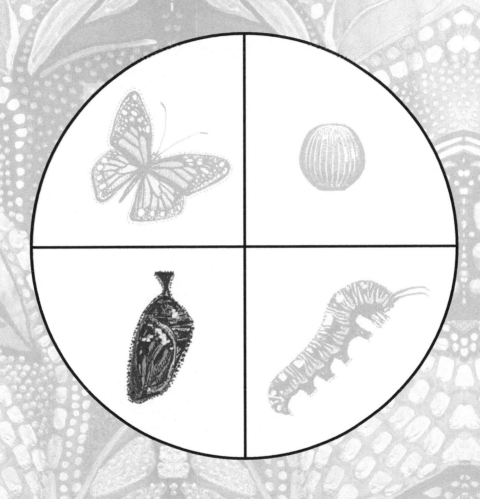

cocoon

**_Let go_ of everything that is no longer you
Release old patterns and cultural
conditioning**

The cocoon phase in *Nature's* metamorphosis process is about letting go. *Allow* what is no longer needed in your life to dissolve. The caterpillar's life is traded in the container of the cocoon.

The caterpillar dissolves into a liquid soup inside the cocoon.

Its future self—t*he butterfly of its own becoming*—eats its former self to nourish the emerging life.

We too must dissolve. We must *Let Go* of all old patterns—everything that is no longer fully alive in us. Nothing is lost, physics tells us, it only changes form.

What is dissolving in us becomes nourishment for our new life.

5 LET GO

Letting go is surrendering to a larger life that's been waiting for us all along. Perhaps for the first time, we are now conscious of our own inner prison. Now we discover the key to our freedom is our ability to release the dead skin of our tattered conditioning. Those former patterns that initially kept us safe, now keep us captive.

Our guiding images can show us the path to our freedom as our dilapidated *Cocoon* dissolves. Now we feel the larger river of life carrying us forward. We are starting to emerge into a new life, with wet wings and yet ready to soar.

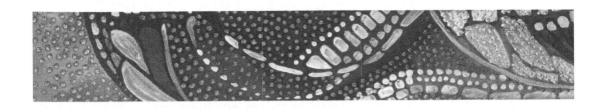

5 LET GO

**RELEASE EVERYTHING YOU ARE NOT
NOURISH WITH IMAGES AND INTUITION**

As I mentioned before, my entor, Dr. Jonas Salk, often said, "let intuition be your guide, with reason by its side." He felt he was primarily an artist and secondarily a scientist because he was led by his intuition and inner images. He would wake up at all times of the night and write from his intuitive self. He solved the riddle to the polio vaccine by imagining himself to be poliovirus itself in the human body. He knew it so well that he then could imagine how to defeat it because he saw it. His intuition, direct perception without rational thought and interference, experienced a deeper truth about the poliovirus. With reason, he then proceeded to create a vaccine to combat the horrific virus.

How might intuition guide your life path now? What if you could spontaneously and directly see your authentic journey with eyes unclouded by your past misperceptions of yourself? How do you cleanse your lenses of perception to see more clearly? How do you develop your intuition as a guide in your life while you also navigate with reason "by its side?"

"In silence there is eloquence.
Stop weaving and watch
how the pattern improves . . .
Your task is not to seek for love,
but merely to seek and find
all the barriers within yourself
that you have built against it."

~Rumi

Letting go is an essential part of change. In Rumi's poem, he tells us to "*Stop* weaving and watch how the pattern improves." *Stopping* is *letting go*. The caterpillar lets go of his former life and *transforms* into a cocoon. Then the cocoon is *let go* when the butterfly emerges. Rumi's directive to "find all the barriers within yourself that you have built against it [love]" is like our *Cocoon* skin that must dissolve into becoming our emerging, fresh, alive authentic self.

"When I let go of what I am, I become what I might be. When I let go of what I have, I receive what I need."

~Lao Tzu

Surrendering to your larger life

Let me tell you the story of Sue Thompson who came to my office on her 49th birthday. "I am giving myself this session as a birthday gift. I am not ready for this birthday. I know things need to change in my life, in my career, and in my marriage. I am confused and frustrated. Every time I try to step forward in my life situation, it seems I end up moving two steps backward instead."

Her *Butterfly* drawing revealed a guiding symbol she called "Fresh Wind" (see drawing on next page). The left drawing of her current position was called "Anger Stuck," which wasn't a surprise for Sue. She told me the following story about this side of her drawing:

"My box is very tight, very contained, yet there are these razor sharp things around me that cut anyone who gets too close to me. That's funny; I never really saw that about myself. I always felt the anger was coming from others, but I now see how angry I am when people try and get near my box."

anger stuck   Fresh wind

We talked about how dense the lines are drawn on her *Cocoon* "Anger stuck" side were, especially in contrast to the image she intuitively drew of her own becoming. Her *Butterfly* image, "Fresh Wind" brought a sense of wonder and mystery to Sue.

"My *Butterfly* drawing is light and open. It is a natural place of freedom. It reminds me of bareboat sailing in the Caribbean last year. A small group of us on the 35-foot sailboat simply let the winds take us, guiding us to our next island. It was uncomfortable sometimes because I wanted to map a course for us, but the group just laughed at me. The islands were so close together, and we just followed the wind and watched for land."

I asked Sue what the message or guidance might be for her current situation. "Trust my path," she said without hesitation. "What is your path now, Sue?" She was silent for a very long time, gazing at the spiral image on her paper. "I am not exactly sure, but like my Caribbean sailing experience, I need to *Let Go* and find a new kind of navigational equipment. Will you guide me?"

I have learned to let the client discover his or her own work to be done. The creative process as a path is very curvy and spiral-like. Her guiding image was a spiral. She was letting go of a heavy box filled with stuck stuff. So I returned the question to her, "How would you guide yourself, Sue?"

Sue again was silent and closed her eyes for a long time. "I see the Fresh Wind symbol in my mind's eye. I was on the sailing vessel in the Caribbean and felt the sea and the feeling when the wind shifts. It was beautiful. I am still not sure how to use this symbol and story in my life, but I feel I am getting clearer and closer than I have been in a long time."

We talked about her vision and sensory rich memory of sailing as the wind shifted. Her homework assignment was to write, stream of consciousness style, looking at both sides of the drawing and writing for about 10 minutes each.

Over the course of her initial sessions, she refined her ability to use the creative Process as a Path in her life. "At first, I couldn't relate to your Process as Path ideas, Dr. Longworth. But then I just kept going back to the image of Fresh Wind. I noticed then that I wouldn't feel lost and alone. As a secondary school teacher, I've been trained to take charge of chaos in my classroom through rational rules and tough consequences. Now I am starting to see how much of that teacher training has influenced the way I am with myself. Keeping a journal of our journey together, as you suggested, has been powerful."

"My primary inner teacher is my belly!" Sue laughed in our last session together. "My belly can feel Fresh Wind when it blows. My creative process is to *Stop* when I realize I am doing something the old '*Cocoon*' way with my box and razors ready to harm anyone who gets close to me. I literally *Stop* and close my eyes for a few minutes. Sometimes I will call in "Fresh Wind." Other times, I will simply *Stop* and be silent, awaiting a feeling or image to inform my life. Sometimes writing in my journal can give me more insight."

"I have come to trust my creativity when I take the time to tune into it. I keep my teacher self at school during classroom hours. I try and do the best I can to then be open to my intuition, or as you speak of it, my creative Process as Path. I find it's helpful to have my *Cocoon* and *Butterfly* images and stories about them to work creatively within my imagination."

Years later, I heard back from Sue. The school system she taught at, due to budget cuts, had offered her an early retirement with full benefits. She jumped at the chance and now spends half of the year in—you guessed it, the Caribbean.

"Having my symbol and story of who I was becoming really helped me make the change I needed to make. It wasn't overnight, it actually took over a year, but I am living a more authentic life now than ever before. And it's funny, I see spirals wherever I go, reminding me to trust my process."

"Some of us think that holding on makes us strong, but sometimes it is letting go."

~Hermann Hesse

Releasing your dead *Cocoon* skin

We may go through many cycles of trying to *Let Go* until finally, we are able to make the big release and *Let Go* of our old ways. The flow of life is powerful and using the Letting Go technique can help you get in the sweet spot of the river so you flow with a larger life, empowering you to *Let Go* of old patterns that no longer serve you.

Often in our lives, we continually go through small *Let Go* experiences. For instance, on the same day last week, I found out my best friend in high school was in hospice, weeks away from dying of cancer, and another older friend died of a heart attack the day before. Without realizing it, I went into a dark funk, the black hole of my *Cocoon*. I was on a writing retreat and mid-way through my second day, I felt like a black fog had descended over my soul. I wasn't able to shake it with all of my tools, so I went for a 2-hour hike in the surrounding wilderness and then did a *Cocoon to Butterfly* drawing.

I knew the solution was to shift into the *Butterfly* metaphor, but it took awhile for me to do it. My *Cocoon to Butterfly* writing revealed that I was ruminating on my pain, obsessed with the reflections of the world that showed me a dark reality. Loneliness, despair, "I have to work for love," friends not showing up, etc. The pattern of my childhood wounds.

Letting Go finally occurred when I clearly saw the light of my *Butterfly Self*. I know that service and structure are an integral part of how I take care of myself, and I had been indulging in no structure and self-pity. So I *Let Go* by choosing to take care of myself with a structured workday of service. I went to sleep by 9 pm that evening so I could get up at 5 am, the optimum time for me to start the day. The soot of my dark *Cocoon* fell away as I began my early morning with my work, redesigning a Women's Support Group flyer. Hours later at the gym, I ran into Suzy Anderson, a student of mine from UCSD. We rejoiced in reuniting again after 18 years since we had seen each other. Then 5 minutes later, as I was leaving, I ran into the director of the facility who invited me to lead a workshop in a few months. Boom! The light of my *Butterfly Self* was shining brightly. Life gave me opportunities for service and joy right away. I needed to be with my own grief, I accepted that I was stuck in the darkness of my *Cocoon* for a few days.

It is important for me to *Allow* myself some space, when the darkness comes, to not be afraid of it. Or judge myself to not be as enlightened or advanced spiritually, because I descend into the darkness of my soul. There can be a lot of misled beliefs in the spiritual community about being awake or enlightened. Something must be very wrong if you aren't in joy or peacefully centered all the time. The reality of life is that it is always moving and changing, like a river. When we *Let Go* into it, sometimes it takes us down an eddy that has us *Stop* on a shore for a while. Our experience can feel like being stuck in mucky mud. But if we *Allow* ourselves the experience and stay in *Let Go*, it moves. The experience of our traveling makes us a wiser person.

Guiding images show you the path

The devastating day my first marriage ended, something happened that gave me tremendous strength. Spontaneously, I went into my art studio and grabbed an old deer antler trophy off the wall. Then without a single thought, holding an antler in each hand, I tore the two apart. The loud crack of the skull ripping open matched the feeling of the container of my

14. Lisa Longworth

5-year relationship being torn apart. Then, in the next hour, with the supplies in my art studio the antlers themselves become a sculpture.

Intuitively, I had chosen to create a *Butterfly* power object from the death of my marriage. The *Cocoon* had clearly perished, the marriage was finished. I had no idea how I would reconstruct my new life. When I *Listened* deeply, the *Butterfly* of my own *Becoming* art piece told me its name was Warrior Crown. At that moment when I was completely devastated by the death of the most precious thing in m life, my marriage, this *Butterfly* image would be a lifeboat to carry me safely forward on my journey.

The 3-months I remained in our old home, the Warrior Crown was placed in the center of the house. We put our marriage certificate and other old artifacts of our former life under the sculpture. When I was feeling defeated, I would go to it and place my hand on the base for strength. It worked. Now, ten years later, this Warrior Crown still gives me powerful energy.

15. Lisa Longworth

The art of Letting Go

Unpacking my grandmother's 100-year-old teapot, placing it next to a favorite stained-glass butterfly, I would never have imagined minutes later that both would come crashing to the floor. One of my canvases literally fell off the wall and shattered those two precious possessions into scattered glass shards on the floor.

This was February 21st, the first week in my new home as a freshly divorced woman. Immediately, without thinking, I took the beautiful broken shards of glass and went into my second art studio in the kitchen and put them together. Above is the resulting sculpture.

Holding this beautiful creation in my hands, I saw it as my own life. The "picture" of my life had fallen off the wall, and precious life dreams had "shattered." In the last months, when my husband and I decided to divorce, my heart had been very painfully cut and "broken open." Beauty *Stopped* my mind as I held this sculpture in my hand. I realized in that moment the necessity for life to break us open again and again.

From my own creative process, I learned that beauty is created again and again, often through shattering our most precious dreams. Life is breaking us open to what is fresh and alive now.

My lifework was singing to me, "Lisa, trust life. Remember *Cocoon to Butterfly*, break open again and again and fly!"

Exercise: Recognizing barriers that keep you stuck

Where do you feel stuck now? It will be important to articulate that in both words and images. Use this exercise as a method to move through barriers:

Write: Take 10 minutes and write about feeling stuck or frustrated. Share about your situation and your feelings. Then reread your words and underline one or two words or phrases that have the most juice for you. The ones that express power or intensity are the ones to underline.

Draw: Now find a blank sheet of paper (such as 8.5" by 11" printer paper) and some colored pencils or felt tip pens. You will eventually need 2 pieces of paper the same size if possible. Start with the first piece of paper, and draw the frustration you wrote about. Draw, not as an artist, but simply scribble on the page, to get the energy out.

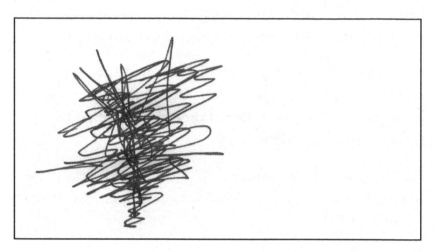

When you recognize that you are running an old pattern, whether it is a thought pattern or a behavior, the most powerful thing you can do is to *Stop*, refocus and release.

In the *Stopping*, you are in silence. Recall the words of Rumi's poem: "In silence there is eloquence." This is a powerful statement. You can articulate to yourself, within your inner silence.

Certain things will trigger you. You will automatically go into the coping mechanism, the safe *Cocoon* skin within your psyche, created for your survival. But it is a barrier against the truth, the truth of your own essential self, the *Butterfly* of your own *Becoming*. For you to evolve, you must release your stuck dead *Cocoon* skin.

Check-In: *Let go*

Use this check-in to help you develop your signature practice and deepen your *transformational* process. Write your answers to the questions in your *C2B Journal* or discuss in your *Cocoon to Butterfly* group.

1. Did you do the exercise, "Recognizing Barriers That Keep You Stuck?"

2. Did you write in your *C2B Journal* this week? If yes, what insights did you receive? If not, do you have insights now?

3. How is your signature practice evolving?

Did you know?

When the adult butterfly initially emerges, its wings are deflated, wrinkled and wet, and the abdomen is distended with fluid. The butterfly then pumps some of the fluid into the wings to inflate them. Then it rests and lets the wings dry out. There will be no growth during this fourth cycle of its life, its primary purpose is to mate and reproduce. Can you believe butterflies have been around since dinosaurs roamed the earth?

the *Cocoon to Butterfly* process
Butterfly = TRANSFORM

butterfly

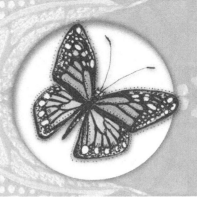

Transform **through Simplicity,**
Play and Gratitude

Although our metamorphosis is often invisible to the outer world, inside we have a newfound freedom.

6 SIMPLIFY

We have learned how important it is to *simplify* all complications by being *Present*. We do whatever is in front of us with our full attention, trusting our larger life to guide us.

7 TRANSFORM

The butterfly has emerged and freely flies in the colorful garden of life. We now live in the joyful freedom of our awakened heart and are ready to live life freely with love, from higher awareness.

6 SIMPLIFY

TRANSFORM BY DOING LESS
SIMPLIFY, SIMPLIFY, SIMPLIFY

**"Our life is frittered away by detail...
simplify, simplify."**

~Henry David Thoreau

"Simplicity is the ultimate sophistication."

~Leonardo da Vinci

**"Simplicity is the law of Nature for men
as well as for flowers."**

~Henry David Thoreau

"Simplify, simplify, simplify"

The problem today is that our lives tend to be complex
and full of just too much. Too much on our calendars,
too many things in our garages, too many projects on
our list, and we are pulled in too many directions. In

too many things in our garages, too many projects on our list, and we are pulled in too many directions. In practice, how do we make things simpler? This chapter is dedicated to exploring our cultural and personal tendency towards complexity and envisioning how we might transform.

Tip:

Do less. Thoreau recommended, "Simplify, simplify, simplify." Don't be seduced into activity. Daily attention to no more than 2 or 3 concerns. Focus on their completion, releasing the rest.

From confusion to peace

The act of *simplifying* our lives is a necessary practice to live a deeply authentic life. It's a journey, not a destination—important to remember! *Simplifying* our lives is an important creative spiritual practice that brings peace from chaos and confusion. It helps to keep the essential quality of our own nature in the forefront, as one stays *Present* in their life moment to moment.

We must *Let Go* and shed old ways to accept new, *transforming* challenges. This principle is a call to practice *simplicity* to focus on what matters most now.

Making your complicated simple

So how do you *simplify* a busy professional life? Many of

my clients are busy professionals juggling many hats. Joanne Duffy was such a person—a well-groomed 59-year old account executive for a top Wall Street Firm. She came into my office complaining about her boss. "He is relentlessly demanding. No matter how much I produce, no matter how well I organize my team, he wants more."

Joanne, whose presence commanded respect, had a creamy white complexion, with skin that looked 10 years younger than her age, in contrast to her soft-centered, stocky body. She wore a periwinkle colored Marie St. John knit dress that set off her twinkly blue eyes. At this point in her life, Joanne was happily single. She divorced at 45 and was childfree. Joanne said, "I am so lucky to choose to live my life my way." Yet she wasn't happy.

Joanne spoke about her 10-hour days at the office, plus she was available to her boss and co-workers almost 24/7 on her cell phone. "I have to keep busy all the time just to keep up with my team's sales quota. And the industry continues to change. It's crazy. But I am stuck. I love my salary, and I am too old now to try and find another job in this marketplace."

Her *Cocoon* drawing (see next page)was entitled "Chaos, Continual" and showed whirling circles within circles. There was a center point and moving lines and circles surrounded it. The *Butterfly* of her own *Becoming* drawing was entitled "Calm Center" and had a central circle

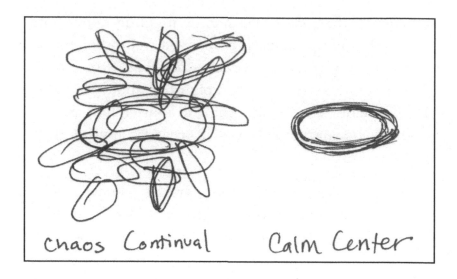

chaos Continual   Calm Center

that looked more like a dew drop surrounded by three half-circles that seemed to hold the dew drop center.

When I asked Joanne to tell me about her drawing, she said, "This is my daily life, "Chaos Central," the phone is always ringing, someone is in distress that needs to be rescued. I am caught up in it all, so I don't have time to think about myself, only the problem at hand. Yet it's very dark inside here," she pointed to the center circle. "There is no peace. It is lonely if I let myself feel it. But most of the time it's too busy. There is too much going on to feel how I am feeling."

Then she told me about the *Butterfly* of her own *Becoming* drawing. "I am sure my inner work is reflected in those three lines," she pointed to the three "U" shaped lines surrounding the center circle. "See how simple those are!" she exclaimed sounding a little like a joyful child, uncharacteristic of her demeanor. "This would be my ideal work life and daily life. Three details to attend to, to focus on; and then I could be calm."

The basic story in Joanne's drawings showed a *transformation* occurring in the area surrounding herself, the center circle of her drawing. When I asked her how she might move from her *Cocoon* to her *Butterfly*, she paused for a long time while gazing thoughtfully at her drawing. "My work life needs to change," she finally said. "OK Joanne, what needs to change in your work life?" I asked, hoping to inspire her to go deeply into herself. "Well," she said slowly with her slight Southern accent, "I need to deal with all these other chaotic strands differently," pointing to her *Cocoon* drawing.

"I want to live a different kind of life now. I can't go on like this anymore." Joanne committed to starting the *Cocoon to Butterfly* program in that moment. We planned her homework together right away. I understood her pattern of overwork and chaos as an avoidance tactic, a major issue to work on in our sessions together, so I brought that up immediately. She said, "Hmm. I guess that might be an issue, I don't know. I am willing to work on it."

Joanne's daily practice began with a *C2B Journal* she would write in upon awakening each morning. She would set her smartphone timer for 20 minutes and then write continually, stream of consciousness writing,

"Simplicity is the ultimate sophistication."

~Leonardo da Vinci

anything and everything that came up. She could not be interrupted.

Five weeks into our sessions, I suggested that her daily practice includes meditation, 10-minutes in the morning and night. She could choose from the *Freedom Meditation, Butterfly Breathing, Entering Presence* or traditional meditation. She could choose some exercise, such as a 10-minute walk in a beautiful setting. The point was to get her to move and also not be interrupted.

After many sessions with discussions about how the chaos of her work life allowed her to avoid dealing with her own life or her own feelings, she began to realize the validity of these avoidance patterns. We talked about this protection as *"Cocoon* skin" to keep her from facing uncomfortable feelings.

My initial vision of Joanne's potential to simplify her life and find more inner peace was a large one. At the end of our work together, she was able to make a small step in changing her life. She now had instant access to find a peaceful place inside of her through the tools she was using in daily practice. But I had hoped, for her sake, she would reclaim a stronger sense of who she was outside of her career identity. In our last session, I realized that it probably would be a longer process than the few months we had worked together for Joanne to truly realize "The Calm Center."

Curiously enough, during the last weeks of our work, her firm offered her a promotion to lead a larger group of people. She told me she felt fortified from our work together, so she could accept more work responsibility without getting pulled down into "Chaos, Continual." My gut feeling was that the seduction of the work and the outer success it brought was a stronger pull for her than the pull to authentically embrace her deeper self and the inner peace that would bring. So we discussed the seduction of work and money in her life now. Was she trading in her inner peace for outer success? Joanne said no. She wanted to ride the wave of her work.

Joanne claims she will continue her signature practice of daily writing and meditation. She's excellent at her work from the firm's point of view and, including her bonuses, makes more than half a million dollars a year. Still, as she left my office, I wondered how much of her "calm center" she had really *allowed* herself to feel. She emailed me a few weeks later excited to be planning a big bash for her 60th birthday on a yacht with over 100 "friends" attending. I pondered her words and wondered if the simplicity of inner peace was still a priority for her.

"Simplicity is the nature of great souls."

~Papa Ramadas

I use the example of Joanne in this chapter on the topic of *Simplifying* because it truly is a difficult task for many people, especially successful professionals. Busy outer activity with all the excitement it brings can be intoxicating. Because our society values external productivity and the accumulation of things as a symbol of success, it is easy to become unconsciously drunk from it. Hopefully, the popularity of mindfulness and yoga today are signs our culture is evolving.

"Making the simple complicated is commonplace; making the complicated simple, awesomely simple, that's creativity."

~Charles Mingus

Exercise: Write about *simplifying* life

Write in your *C2B Journal.* Set your timer for 5 minutes. Write as fast as you can about your benefits in staying busy and keeping your life complex. Then do 5 minutes of the *Butterfly Breathing* exercise (see chapter 2). Now write for 5 minutes, again setting your timer, and writing as fast as you can about your life in the future when you have mastery in exercising simplicity. Remember, you are writing about your future self and your ability to easily *simplify* your daily life.

How do you develop a practice to *simplify*? Here are 6 Tips on how to *simplify*:

1. Eliminate all but what is essential.

2. Spend your time doing what is important to YOU.

3. Identify your most important top 3-5 priorities or values.

4. Evaluate your time and tasks—are they in alignment with your priorities?

5. Develop the muscle of saying no. You'll free up time to do what you love.

6. *Simplify* every day by writing down the 3 most important things to do.

Exercise: From multitasking to simplicity

A mindfulness practice can make you more aware of what is happening right now without judging it. As busy people, we may be unconscious of how multitasking degrades our awareness and our ability to bring the presence and principles of simplification into our lives. Recent research continues to confirm that multitasking increases stress and feelings of being psychologically and physically overburdened. It is a cherished myth that multitasking increases our productivity and it has been proven false. Yet, multitasking still seduces us...

1. Would you be willing to make a commitment to not multitask for one week (if not a week, a day), as an experiment?

2. If so, write out your commitment to yourself in your journal. Such as, what you will do, time frame, taking notes about what you discover in your journal, your intention (more peace, more clarity for example).

3. If you've been multitasking for a long time, the pattern change may be challenging. Be mindful of everything that arises as you attempt to create this new pattern of simplicity over multitasking.

4. If you find that the experiment of simplicity over multitasking is working, will you choose to make it your new lifestyle? Is it part of becoming your future *Butterfly Self*?

Check-in: *Simplify*

Use this check-in to help you develop your signature practice and go deeply into your *transformational* process. Write your answers to the questions in your *C2B Journal* or discuss in your *Cocoon to Butterfly* group.

1. Did you write in your *C2B Journal* about simplifying your life?

2. Did you make any commitments to yourself around multi-tasking? What did you notice?

3. What opens up for you as you simplify your life?

4. How is your signature practice evolving? Are you experiencing any blocks?

7 TRANSFORM

FREEDOM AND JOY IN HIGHER AWARENESS
PLAY, GRATITUDE & GENEROSITY

"It is only with the heart, that one can see rightly, what is invisible to the eye."

~Antoine de Saint-Exupery

"It is a happy talent to know how to play."

~Ralph Waldo Emerson

"Follow your bliss and the universe will open doors where there were only walls."

~Joseph Campbell

Emerging from your *Cocoon* feeling fresh

Now that you are unstuck from dead layers of your *Cocoon* skin, are you feeling in a fresh place of *transformation* now? A lightness of being?

Your higher consciousness emerging

Often your higher consciousness emerges with this new freedom. The beauty of life is seen more clearly. Also, a sense of effortless ease is felt. The creative tension has fallen away for now. You are the butterfly frolicking among vivid flowers in the garden of your life. Joy of joys!

In the majority of *Cocoon to Butterfly* drawings I have witnessed in my practice, the *Butterfly* drawings are always more expansive and airy than the *Cocoon* drawings. Your *Butterfly Self* plays in freedom. It has escaped the stuck place of the *Cocoon's* prison.

Leela, your conscious playful self

The ancient Sanskrit word "Leela" means "play." Not ordinary play, but Play on an elevated level of higher consciousness. From this perspective, the world of form can be witnessed as a theater of consciousness. A stage where life as we see it and experience it is part of a cosmic dance, a divine Play. We have a spiritual perspective now.

My brush with death after brain surgery allowed me to see myself from a larger perspective. I saw that I was not only an individual but also a whole living system, the fully conscious earth in an awakening universe. I like to call it the awakened heart.

Your awakened heart, your true nature

Transforming into your new life, you have wings at last! A freedom is felt from this new beautiful territory of your authentic self. Where there once was confusion, there is now clarity—your consciousness feels clean and vast.

Perhaps you awoke from a terrible dream of being alone and separate. In this connectedness of your heart to all things, there is peace. Meditation brings you deeper into the awakened heart and into feeling your true nature shining forth.

Now that you have tasted life from your expanded self, the *Butterfly* of your own *Becoming*, you know a level of this freedom. You can make a deeper commitment to always live from this awakened place.

"The creation of something new is not accomplished by the intellect but by the play instinct."

~Carl Jung

Your *Butterfly Self* plays in freedom

Finally, there is time for play in this *Butterfly* stage. We discover how easy it is to cultivate the spirit of fun while being *Present*. In this stage, you will feel more creative flow and less effort and hard work.

The degree to which you feel authentic flow in your life is in equal measure to the amount of joy and freedom you are likely to experience. A shift can take place where you view your life from a higher, wider perspective, and discover new ways of thinking and creating. The culmination of this journey brings a sense of gratitude and an eagerness to contribute more to life, both within and around you.

The spirit of Play is one of the most important qualities you can recover as an adult. This chapter is at the end of the book because we have been conditioned to work for what we want, and Play can be challenging to access. Yet the spirit of Play lubricates and lightens those heavy wheels of responsibility that can make our daily achievement machines feel burdened.

Playing as meditation

Play is an invitation to be in the *Present* moment. Traditional meditation, the Eastern kind where one sits with their eyes closed, is fabulous. It helps build the mental muscle to keep the mind chatter from dominating one's inner life. The art of playing can also be a powerful meditation. It is difficult for the noise of the mind chatter to dominate when you are playing.

You cultivate the spirit of fun with ease

The great thing about Play is it's fun! Playing naturally brings joy and levity.

In our busy lives, we carry so many responsibilities, it's hard to let them go and give ourselves the freedom to Play. Our culture programs us to work more than to Play... Do you live to work or work to live? We Americans tend to do the former. I believe our European neighbors work to live. The average American takes off ten days a year, with one in four taking no vacations at all. The average European takes thirty days. In your *Cocoon to Butterfly* process, if you are living to work, this may be an old *Cocoon* skin you want to shed.

Your spirit of play lightens and lubricates responsibility

Many geniuses "work" all the time, but truly their work is their Play. Scientists, artists, writers, inventors, etc., may be in continual exploration of their work, but the spirit from which they are driven is different than what we are talking about here. You know who you are!

I recently finished a London radio interview where the first question I was asked was "why do Americans have such a hard time taking vacation time?" Can you relate to this challenge? I responded to the question by saying Americans are deeply patterned to achieve and get ahead by working hard. It's in our cultural DNA. We are rooted in the Protestant work ethic, which believes that it is your duty to achieve success through hard work, discipline, and thrift, with such success being a sign you are saved. Is your work "saving" you or keeping you stuck in your *Cocoon*?

"I am thankful for laughter, except when milk comes out of my nose."

~Woody Allen

Exercise: Youngster yoga (for play)

Hang out with children. Watch how they Play, laugh and move. Breathe deeply and connect with that child's spirit. You can go to a playground. Offer to babysit a child. Find photographs in magazines of children that bring joy to you, and make a collage to put in your Sacred Place at home. Collect fun stickers to spontaneously give to children when you see them.

Exercise: Laughter yoga (for play)

Laughter Yoga, (Hasya Yoga), have you heard of it? The "workout" is laughing continuously. It is based on the theory that voluntary laughter provides the same benefits as spontaneous laughter. Generally laughter yoga is done in groups in person; however, online laughter clubs where you can make contact through the phone can be just as effective. Search online for "laughter yoga, phone" and you will find many organizations that offer their services without charge. You can also simply laugh out loud by yourself for 30 seconds and find that the forced laughter turns into real and contagious laughter. It's really fun. Try it!

Exercise: Islands of time to play

Create open fields of time on your schedule. Starting with as little as 10 minutes up to several hours, try to explore the most **"islands of time to play"** you can open up on your calendar. *Allow* your natural rhythm and flow to have space.

- Be spontaneous! Play does not have a definite beginning or end.
- Take small breaks in between tasks, for example, 10–15 minutes after an hour of focused productive activity.
- *Stop* where you are and ask your inner self, "Where would you like to go? What would you like to do?"
- Consider connecting your playtime to your spiritual practice. Play with lighting candles, incense, making altars, or anything that connects you in a creative way.

- Set up a "playground" in your home with art supplies that can easily be taken down from a shelf for a few minutes of Play. Some have found it helpful to make a Play date list of things that access the spirit of Play.

- Think of three activities that evoke your spirit of Play. Write them down. Do them this week!

Breathe and *Let Go*. Let your mind be still and *Listen*. Be aware of the images that may arise in your mind. *Listen* to the still small voice within. Check to see if you have a positive pull on an arising image. If so, let the pull guide you. Set your timer for the allotted amount of time and then *Let Go* and see what happens.

Robert Wright, a neurosurgeon at Green Hospital in La Jolla, came to me aching to play more music in his life and to resolve some relationship challenges with his wife. His *Cocoon* drawing was of a little figure in a big imposing box with a lot of tension around it. His *Butterfly* drawing had a winged guitar that was sailing in a blue sky with sunshine radiating out of it. He called the *Butterfly* of his own *Becoming* "Freedom" and the *Cocoon* drawing "Entrapped." In his current reality, he felt imprisoned by the demands of his career. The politics of the hospital and his practice demanded long hours with little time to pursue his musical pleasures. His vision of himself playing music, "Freedom," seemed like a pipe dream. He needed things to change because he was starting to "hate" a profession he had always "loved." "I don't want to lose my passion for helping my patients get well. I just have to play music. Can you help me do both?" he asked in our initial session.

He would use the image of his vision, "Freedom," during long board meetings at the hospital when he felt frustrated and bored with his hospital work. While envisioning his winged guitar, he would subtly play the "air guitar" under the boardroom table. When he came in for his weekly session, he shared how new this behavior was for him. Previously he would just feel frustrated and hopeless with his physician role at the hospital, but now with the *Butterfly* vision, it helped him focus his creative energy towards his dreams. At night when he would return home, he would go to his home office late at night and play with Garage Band on his computer for half an hour before retiring.

It took Robert a few months of holding his *Butterfly* vision while in the current reality of his *Cocoon* "trapped" before he experienced much outer movement. He confessed that he had doubts about our work together. He had doubts about himself and his ability to be a musician and a full-time physician, but he kept his images close to his heart and used them to stay connected to his musical dreams. One session, he walked into my office and handed me a CD. "This is my first album! I did it!"

He had made a breakthrough releasing the feeling of being trapped in his career at the hospital. He also embraced the uncomfortable feelings of the creative tension between his career and having time to be musical. The concept of an organic creative tension in the creative process was new to him. Before, he felt creative tension but put it in the category of stress, the fight or flight kind that makes adrenaline and cortisol surge in the body. Unconsciously he had decided he could be a doctor or a musician, but not both. He came to realize the creative tension between the doctor work and guitar work could actually be a very positive force in his life to creating music.

His relationship with his wife improved as well because he wasn't as frustrated at work. He accepted her personality more fully. There was work to do, and we again looked for images that supported Robert's current reality or *Cocoon* self and his *Butterfly* vision of what was next.

Robert would continue to work with his new images for this next cycle of growth with his wife. I suggested he create a *C2B Journal*, with his *Cocoon to Butterfly* images and stories. He initially scoffed at adding "yet one more thing" to his very busy schedule. He enjoyed getting up early and committed to a minimum of 10 minutes of writing first thing every morning while drinking his coffee in his den.

His journal process revealed his old *Cocoon* skin survival-oriented coping mechanism that kept him in a "safe" distance from his wife. That *Cocoon* had become an emotional prison for Robert, and he began to realize he was actually numb to much of his wife's feelings.

Psychology tells us that we build barriers against pain. Our magnificent psyche makes a safe container for us to survive when we need to. Like building a *Cocoon*, it *allows* us to develop and grow up. We don't die at four years old when a parent rages at us. These reactive patterns or coping mechanisms keep us safe for a while.

You may be able to survive by flying away to a safe place in your imagination or building barriers to not feel overwhelming pain, but eventually, the comforting pattern becomes a prison, for which you must discover the key to escape. It is time to find the barriers, the dead *Cocoon* skins of your former self and prepare to release them.

GRATITUDE

"Gratitude unlocks the fullness of life. It turns what we have into enough, and more. It turns denial into acceptance, chaos to order, and confusion to clarity. It can turn a meal into a feast, a house into a home, a stranger into a friend. Gratitude makes sense of our past, brings peace for today and creates a vision for tomorrow."

~Melody Beattie

Generosity expands as you become the *Butterfly*

Life is generous. As we change and transform from *Cocoon to Butterfly*, we also become more generous. Our consciousness expands to see a larger perspective and discover new ways of thinking and creating.

"Saying 'thank you' is more than good manners. It is good spirituality."

–Alfred Painter

Exercise: Gratitude through writing

Try having your *C2B Journal* by your bed and write at least 7 to 10 things you're grateful for that day right before you go to bed. You can also use 3 by 5 cards or slips of paper and end the ritual by folding and placing them into a special vase or bowl. If you would rather not write things down on paper, this exercise can be done as you first lie down to go to bed. You can count using your fingers like in the *Butterfly Breathing Meditation* in Chapter 2.

"Feeling gratitude, and not expressing it, is like wrapping a present and not giving it."

~William Arthur Ward

Exercise: Gratitude through speaking

Practice sharing your appreciation for others around you in simple positive statements. You might try starting with "Something I appreciate about you is____." Or, "I am grateful you are in my life." A variation on this practice is looking for beauty wherever you go. When it's with a person then you could say, "You have such beautiful ____."

"'Thank you' is the best prayer that anyone could say. I say that one a lot. Thank you expresses extreme gratitude, humility, understanding."

~Alice Walker

Exercise: Gratitude in random moments

Take random moments during the day to *Stop*, close your eyes when possible, and experience gratitude.

When you witness your mind chatter obsessing on some topic, *Stop* and express gratitude to life. By simply witnessing the mind stream and saying "thank you," your inner peace is strengthened. Your inner word of "thank you" fortifies your *Butterfly* wings as you move through your life.

Go to your inner Place of Peace and have that be a place to express gratitude. You may consider creating a special place just to express gratitude. For instance, your Place of Peace (see Chapter 2) might be the seashore and in contrast, your Place of Gratitude might be a mountain cavern or a temple. In your Place of Gratitude, you can simply say "thank you" or find yourself giving thanks in other ways such as a dance.

"The essence of all beautiful art is gratitude."

~Friedrich Nietzsche

Exercise: Gratitude through art and movement

Make something as an expression of gratitude. It could be a collage cutting out magazine images and pasting them on paper. Or you could make something from clay, wood, or paint. The most important factor is to remember that you are creating this as an expression of gratitude, not as you might make a piece of art. It is a way to give gratitude.

Consider doing a Dance of Gratitude. You could do this privately somewhere that feels good to you in your home or out in *Nature*. Find a perfect piece of music and use the length of it to create the structure of time you will dance. While dancing, stay focused on the gratitude you are expressing and *Let Go* of any self-consciousness you may feel. Fully experience and receive the gift of gratitude that you have expressed after your dance. Imagine you are a butterfly who has just pollinated many flowers in the dance of life.

Take a Gratitude Walk. Internally say "Thank you" to everything you see as you are walking. For instance, you see a tree and say "thank you," you see a house, a car, a mailbox. Gently feel the gratitude for that thing in your presence, *allowing* whatever you feel or think about to arise. Stay with the process, refocusing your attention when it gets off course. It is an amazing practice to shift from ordinary mind stream thinking to the deep and sacred space of gratitude.

"You simply will not be the same person two months from now after consciously giving thanks each day for the abundance that exists in your life. And you will have set in motion an ancient spiritual law: the more you have and are grateful for, the more will be given you."

~Sarah Ban Breathnach

Exercise: For your *Butterfly* life

Pause first, as you change into your new life: As the brand new butterfly emerges freshly from its cocoon, it doesn't instantaneously fly away into its new life. Slowly the delicate butterfly pumps fluid into its wet wings and then it must dry before it's ready to take flight. So too, when you begin to live in your freedom, the old patterns of your *Cocoon* may want to take hold. *Stop* briefly, like the emerging butterfly, and check in with your essential self before you automatically move forward.

Journal Your Gratitude: Get out your *C2B Journal* and express your gratitude through writing. You can make a list of what you are grateful for in this moment and you can also write a letter to the Universe (Life, Source, or God), and have Gratitude for what you've been given. This is especially powerful to do when feeling in a funky, dark place. Even though initially you may not feel the gratitude, the act of expressing gratitude will make you feel better.

Nature Time: Spending time in *Nature* is essential to your well being. Find a way, every day, to go outside and connect to plants, sky, and earth. Make a ritual of watching the sunrise or sunset, being aware of the moon cycles, and gaze at the stars whenever possible. Make a commitment to spend extended time in a natural place that feeds your soul. Write about spending time in *Nature* in your *C2B Journal.* Walking in *Nature* is great. Put it on your calendar. If you can't get out in *Nature*, bring it with you. Place a flowering plant next to your computer and remember to take breaks to simply gaze at it, or smell it, or feel the dirt it is growing in. Perhaps you could even feel its leaves on your cheek. Embrace *Nature* and be fed by it.

Solitude Time: If you are often surrounded by people at work and at home, creating solitude time in your life may be essential to keeping your new wings strong and healthy. Go somewhere by yourself for a retreat. It could be camping, a cabin, a hotel, or an all day drive somewhere beautiful. The key is to stay quiet and be with yourself. This is a perfect time to write and draw in your journal or read uplifting books. You can also create solitude time while you live with others through agreement. For instance, "I would like to spend this evening, from 7 to 9 pm, in the den by myself. Would that work for you?" Be mindful of how it feels to take solitude.

Check-in: *Transform & Gratitude*

Use this check-in to help you develop your signature practice and go deeply into your *transformational* process. Write your answers to the questions in your *C2B Journal* or discuss in your *Cocoon to Butterfly* group.

1. Were you able to give yourself some time for creative Play?

2. Which gratitude exercise did you find most helpful and why?

3. How is your signature practice evolving? Are you experiencing any blocks?

16. Lisa Longworth

"Play is an expression of gratitude for
the great gift of life."

~Br. David Steindl-Rast

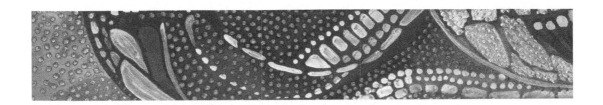

CONCLUSION

**"You have no control over how your story begins
or ends. But by now, you should know
that all things have an ending.
Every spark returns to darkness.
Every sound returns to silence.
Every flower returns to sleep with the earth.
The journey of the sun and moon is predictable.
But yours, is your ultimate art."**

~Suzy Kassem,

Rise Up and Salute the Sun

The end is a space just before the beginning—the butterfly lays eggs!

We have reached the end of this book, but not the end of your process. Like cycles of the moon, you will continue to go through cycles of change for the rest of your life. Most people go through at least 3 to 5 big changes in their lives. As you know, midlife changes can often inspire a deeper, more soulful search for creating meaning and redefining values.

This last section is here to restate the main tools to remember from this book. Take these jewels to work with right now as you begin your *Cocoon to Butterfly* journey.

Have you chosen cupcakes or creative change?

Do you remember the photo of the cupcake at the beginning of the book, (on page 18), with the question posed to you, "Are you going to have cupcakes or creative change?"

The idea of eating cupcakes can be like reading this self-help book for entertainment or amusement, just as you might eat those sweet, yummy, easy to swallow, cupcakes at a birthday party. Creative change requires using tools for your personal *transformation*. Any one of the 24 tools in this book most likely will require your intention, commitment, and discipline to integrate into your daily life.

This is a moment, to check in with yourself and your process in reading this book. Has this book so far been a tool for your *transformation*, or more like a sweet cupcake to consume for entertainment?

Creativity is like a muscle that can be developed and needs exercise. The most important aspect of this book is your Signature Practice.

Remember to keep reinventing your Signature Practice

Hopefully, a couple of the tools in this book have become a part of your daily routine. For some people, it can be important to get a sense of the whole enchilada before actually taking their first bite (or exercise in this case.) Others are nibblers and *Stop* along the way to taste small bites.

Remember your Signature Practice is your custom-designed inner workout to strengthen the muscles of your creativity and connection to your soul. There are two-dozen exercises and tools in this book including meditation, journaling, art and creative spiritual practices; all designed to support your *transformation*. I just can't emphasize enough how important it is to actually do them. Your inner workout needs to be done as consistently as you can.

Inspiration for those who *haven't started* the exercises yet:

1. First, do the *Cocoon to Butterfly* drawing exercise (on page 80) so you have your primary creative change symbols to work with.

2. If there were just one more exercise to do, the *C2B Journal* (on page 36) would be a great choice. It is a most powerful change tool, especially if you can do it on a daily basis. Just use your C2B Journal or a piece of paper and start.

3. If exploring on paper isn't your thing, then review all the other exercises. Find at least one that best supports strengthening the *Butterfly* of your own *Becoming*.

Inspiration for those *who have tried already* an exercise or two:

1. Keep doing the practices and exercises that engage you. *Let go* of exercises that don't.

2. The strongest path to creative change is daily attention to your Signature Practice. Whatever your practice is, it could be one or many practices. Do what works for you. Let it evolve.

3. Keep your commitment to your Signature

Practice. Do it daily, if you miss your routine, start again. Keep it simple and intend for it to support your deepest *transformation.*

Remember to keep discovering your *Cocoon to Butterfly* change images and stories

Your images, symbols, metaphors and stories change as you do. So keep them fresh. The *Cocoon to Butterfly* drawing process (on page 80), once you have done it a few times, will be a practice you can do in a few minutes rather than an hour. The initial images you receive can help you navigate your *transformational* journey, along with the stories the images tell you when you write about them.

Use the *Cocoon to Butterfly* Drawing Process when stressed out or confused

In the future, if you find yourself off balance or out of sorts, get out your pen and paper. Do the *Cocoon to Butterfly* drawing process.

Reviewing the *Cocoon to Butterfly* Drawing Process

1. Use paper and pen, your *C2B Journal*, or a 3 x 5 card.

2. Focused on your challenging feeling or situation (the stuck *Cocoon*), draw a quick scribble of it on the left side.

3. Focused on breaking through the challenge (the *Butterfly* of your own *Becoming*), draw a quick scribble of it on the right side.

4. Name the *Cocoon* image and write it down on the top or bottom of the drawing, then name the *Butterfly* image.

5. Write about the each image, and then read your stories out loud.

6. Feel the creative tension between the *Cocoon* and the *Butterfly* drawings. Look at your drawing from time to time. It is medicine for your *transformational* journey.

Remember the metamorphosis of the *Butterfly* is a map for your journey

If you align with *Nature*, you will align with your own true nature. As you recall, we discussed how the butterfly is *Nature's* most magical changing creature and offers us an organic navigational chart:

Egg = renew/stop our vital energy and meditate

Caterpillar = open/listen to intuition and images

Cocoon = let go/simplify everything that is no longer you

Butterfly = transform, simplicity, play & gratitude

If you find yourself lost remember:

1. **The _Egg_.** Stop and put your attention in the _Present_ moment. You may need to retreat from the world you are currently involved in to rest and refuel yourself. By focusing your attention on some form of meditation you'll renew your vital energy.

2. **The _Caterpillar_.** Nourish yourself by listening to your intuition, images, metaphors, symbols, and stories. Use your images of change and the stories they tell to navigate your path. _Allow_ creative tension to be uncomfortable.

3. **The _Cocoon_.** Guiding images show you the path. _Let go_ of everything that is no longer you by surrendering to your larger life.

4. **The _Butterfly_.** Remember to _Transform_ through play and gratitude. Your life is simple and joyful as you live through this higher awareness.

Remember
your 7 simple change tools

Our seven simple change tools help us shift out of old patterning to follow an authentic river of life's energy.

1. ***Stop & Renew*** *time, space and vital energy*

2. ***Be Present*** *still mind chatter*

3. ***Open*** *to images and intuition*

4. ***Allow*** *creative tension*

5. ***Let Go*** *release everything you are not*

6. ***Simplify*** *do less*

7. ***Transform*** *freedom & joy in higher awareness*

I leave you with my favorite butterfly poem, written over 2,400 years ago. As you fly into the new freedom of the *Butterfly* of your own *Becoming*, you may be asking yourself, who am I now?

"I dreamed I was a butterfly,

flitting around in the sky;

then I awoke.

Now I wonder:

Am I a man who dreamt

of being a butterfly,

or am I a butterfly dreaming

that I am a man?"

~Chuang Tzu

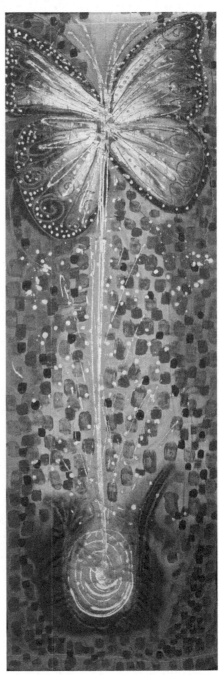

17. Lisa Longworth

Get your copy of the:
Cocoon to Butterfly Journal, A 7-Week proven course to break through life challenges.

For book orders & additional resources
visit our website at
www.lisalongworth.com.

Join our Global *Cocoon to Butterfly* community.

Discover more about private *Cocoon to Butterfly*
sessions with Dr. Longworth by contacting her at
dr@lisalongworth.com

Events described are based on Dr. Longworth's memory of client sessions and experiences. However, the names of all clients discussed in this book have been changed. Additionally, each case with identifying details, such as professions, ages, challenges, etc. have been changed. Any resemblance to persons living or dead resulting from changes to name and identifying details is coincidental. The *Cocoon to Butterfly* drawings contained here have been modified from their original form and recreated.

We wish to acknowledge that the proper scientific term for the butterfly's "cocoon" is chrysalis. However, this book is about healing and breaking free of any prisons within ourselves in order to do so. Dr. Longworth's work since the mid-eighties has been called *Cocoon to Butterfly, Creative Midlife Change*. She has found the metaphor of breaking open our inner cocoon to be very helpful in supporting creative change.

LIST OF ART WORK

Cover: *Golden Butterfly*, Traveling Painting Series, Silk, acrylic, dyes and mix media, Lisa Longworth

1. *Cocoon Womb*, Digital art, Lisa Longworth

2. *Joyful Flight*, Traveling Painting Series, Silk, acrylic, dyes and mix media, Lisa Longworth

3. *Butterfly Bliss*, Silk, paper, mixed media, Lisa Longworth

4. Three photographs from left to right, Thinkstock/Patrik Stedrak. Thinkstock/Doug Chinnery, Thinkstock/Gracie Ross

5. *Cocoon to Butterfly*, Traveling Painting Series, Silk, acrylic, dyes and mixed media, Lisa Longworth

6. *Butterfly Mask*, Mixed media, cloth, acrylic, Lisa Longworth

7. *Reflection in the Cocoon*, Canvas, acrylic paint, mixed media, Lisa Longworth

8. *Mystic Eye*, Canvas, Acrylic paint, mixed media, Lisa Longworth

9. *Birthing New World*, Canvas, acrylic paint, mixed media, Lisa Longworth

10. *Consciousness Rising*, Handmade cast paper, leather, feathers, tree branches, Lisa Longworth

11. *Breathing*, Paper and mixed media, Lisa Longworth

12. *Freedom*, Traveling Painting Series, Silk, acrylic, dyes and mix media, Lisa Longworth

13. *The Eternal Kiss*, Traveling Painting Series, Silk, acrylic, dyes and mix media, Lisa Longworth

14. *Warrior Crown*, Antlers, clay, stones, twine, Lisa Longworth

15. *Shattered Blossom*, Porcelain, glue, Lisa Longworth

16. *Safe Flight*, Silk, mixed media, photographs, paper, Lisa Longworth

17. *Breaking Out*, Traveling Painting Series, Silk, acrylic, dyes and mix media, Lisa Longworth

ACKNOWLEDGEMENTS

I am deeply grateful to many people who make this book possible. And one butterfly. It was a yellow California Dogface butterfly that landed on the back of my hand in 1985. Exactly in that moment, as I was talking on the phone with Jonas Salk, M.D., the words "*Cocoon to Butterfly*" were first whispered to me. Jonas, I am so grateful for the next five years of almost daily dialogues we had on creativity as a healing force to serve the world. Thank you for empowering me to follow my own calling as a creative healer. Thank you to Dr. Dennis Nigro, M.D. who discovered my large brain tumor in 1979, invisible to the 16 other doctors before him who examined me, you trusted your intuition and gave me my life back.

Thank you to my husband, Michael. I am grateful for your encouragement to "just finish" the manuscript without it having to be perfect. Thank you for the gift of editing and inspiration that came from Chad Edwards, Chiwah Slater, Carolyn Johnson, Rod O'Connor and Sarah Jones. And to Stephanie Rogers, who brought inspiration and intelligence to help me finish this book. Thanks to the talented Teri Rider for her publishing expertise and enormous commitment to creating the most beautifully designed book possible. Your wisdom and creativity in this field, combined with your devotion to being my "book baby midwife" made magic happen between its covers.

Stuck in a dark *Cocoon* several times while writing this book, it was my dear friend and author Marion Moss Hubbard, Ph.D. who inspired me to trust the process and *Allow* it to naturally unfold. (Sound familiar?) Your wisdom and encouragement made such a difference. Thank you to my friend, Naomi Call, a consistent champion of the creative birth of this book.

Thank you to my students and clients over the last 3 decades who have taught me about creativity and how the creative process can heal and evolve our consciousness. Together we soar!

About the Author

Dr. Lisa Longworth is a pioneer in the creative process; her *Cocoon to Butterfly*™ program has helped over 15,000 individuals and 4,000 groups through creative metamorphosis in the last 30 years. Her work integrates creativity, psychology, and spirituality.

She is a counselor, artist, speaker, entrepreneur and former university faculty member. A magna cum laude graduate in the arts from UCSD, she holds a masters degree in psychology and a doctorate in psychology. A professional artist since 1975, her paintings have traveled the world with her lectures and workshops. Lisa's near-death experience after life-threatening brain surgery at age 19, continues to inspire her work and daily life. She lives in Southern California with her husband, enjoying every day to the fullest. Her art studio is a living laboratory for both her writing and visual art making. Her current works, "Art as Medicine for *Transformation*," are sculptures about metamorphosis and healing. She travels the world, speaking and teaching, as well as discovering new places, people and cultures that inspire, connect and transform her life.

Made in the USA
Las Vegas, NV
02 November 2021

33573919R00109